THE BIOLOGY OF SUCCESS

THE BIOLOGY OF
SUCCESS

MICHAEL SIMMONS

Charleston, SC
www.PalmettoPublishing.com

The Biology of Success
Copyright © 2023 by Michael Simmons

All rights reserved
No portion of this book may be reproduced, stored in a retrieval system, or transmitted in any form by any means–electronic, mechanical, photocopy, recording, or other–except for brief quotations in printed reviews, without prior permission of the author.

First Edition

Paperback ISBN: 979-8-8229-1345-5
eBook ISBN: 979-8-8229-1345-5

THANK YOU, BETH

"I am an irresistible magnet, with the power to attract unto myself everything that I divinely desire, according to the thoughts, feelings and mental pictures I constantly entertain and radiate. I am the center of my Universe! I have the power to create whatever I wish. I attract whatever I radiate. I attract whatever I mentally choose and accept, I begin choosing and mentally accepting the highest and best in life. I now choose and accept health, success and happiness. I now choose lavish abundance for myself and for all humankind. This is a rich, friendly Universe and I dare to accept its riches, its hospitality, and to enjoy them now."

—Catherine Ponder

For more information, please visit
https://www.youtube.com/@NUTRITIONBIOCHEMISTRY.

Five Pillars to Wealth

1. Get and stay healthy.
2. Focus on what you want.
3. Keep learning.
4. Save 10 percent of your income.
5. Invest in passive income streams.

A Syllabus for Waking the Mind from the Trance of Poverty, Recommended in the Following Order

1. *It Works: The Famous Little Red Book That Makes Your Dreams Come True* by R. H. Jarrett (book)
2. "Prosperity Attracting Money in Speed" by Israel Healing System (audio)
3. *The Secret* starring Rhonda Byrne (video)
4. *Thought Power* by Swami Sivananda (book)
5. *The Power of Your Subconscious Mind* by Joseph Murphy (book)
6. *The Science of Getting Rich* by Wallace Wattles (book)
7. *Think and Grow Rich* by Napoleon Hill (book)

Further Reading

- *The Edinburgh Lectures on Mental Science* by Thomas Troward
- *Healing Is Voltage* by Dr. Jerry Tennant
- *Nutrient Power* by Dr. William J. Walsh
- *Cupid's Poisoned Arrow* by Marnia Robinson
- *Little Book of Common Sense Investing* by Jack Bogle
- *The Intelligent Investor* by Benjamin Graham

Table of Contents

Chapter 1: Destiny and Free Will 1

Chapter 2: Thought and Autosuggestion 7

Chapter 3: Electromagnetic Waves and Telepathy 12

Chapter 4: Stress and Fear 36

Chapter 5: Nutrition 40

Chapter 6: Behavioral Disorders 96

Chapter 7: Behavior and Addiction 100

Chapter 8: Eating Behavior 104

Chapter 9: Sick Building Syndrome 119

Chapter 10: Zoonotic Disease 123

Chapter 11; Psychological Obstacles to Success 129

Chapter 12: Perception and Attraction 138

Chapter 13: Divorce 150

Chapter 14: Sex 154

Chapter 15: Seminal Fluid 161

Chapter 16: Onanism 176

Chapter 17: Coitus Reservatus 181

Chapter 18: Aging and Purpose 184

Chapter 19: Money and Work 191

Chapter 20: Investing in the Stock Market 195

Notes 217

CHAPTER 1:
DESTINY AND FREE WILL

The combination of the law of averages, the law of individual selection, and the law of karma offers people free will under the umbrella of destiny. The law of averages ensures the survival and vitality of the species by balancing growth and survival rates. If all the fish that were born survived until adulthood, they would destroy the oceans through overpopulation. Nature has matched the birth rate of fish with a devastating margin of destruction, preventing overpopulation. The survival rate maintains a balanced fish population. Humans have a much lower birth rate and therefore a higher success rate for the survival of offspring. As the intelligence of the species and individual advances, the law of averages is overshadowed by the law of individual selection. The law of averages places the fate of the individual and the species with outside conditions, while the law of individual selection shifts control to the individual. When individual selection is the governing law, survival is determined by the choices of the individual and their parents in the environment. The law of individual selection provides a species with free will on a personal level.[1]

Human intelligence means that people are ruled by the law of individual selection instead of the law of averages, for the sake of the species' viability and individual success. The law of individual selection essentially comes down to choice, and the law of averages comes down to chance. The influence of each on an individual is variable. There is always an element of chance in any situation outside the control of an individual. However, the more that thought, focus, and preparation go into a decision, the more that chance will wane and choice will wax. These two laws of chance and choice follow the individual through life and are buried in every circumstance and decision. The aggregate sum of seemingly small decisions determines a person's condition in life. All these small decisions defining a person's life pools with the decisions of other individuals. Aggregate population pooling is observed in physical population clusters, such as employment fields and neighborhoods, as well as in social striations, such as day laborers, middle management, upper management, and business owners.

The earth may have a program or growth cycle that eclipses individual choice, making humans part of a larger destiny. The law of averages implies that all individuals of a species are not essential to fulfilling the destiny of that species. The effect of these two laws allows the individual the freedom to pursue their own goals and ambitions under the umbrella of destiny through the law of karma. The law of karma states that actions taken by an individual produce results in kind. The law of karma may also be a safeguard to ensure the destiny of nature. Thoughts, actions, or behaviors that interfere with this larger objective would be curtailed and balanced out through karma. The combination of these three laws protects programmed destiny from misaligned behavior while creating a space for self-expression. Actions that interfere with nature's destiny may produce negative feelings and outcomes that help discourage people from repeating those acts. Conversely, people who help carry out nature's programmed destiny may be filled with a sense of purpose and an increased quality of life because of their actions, creating an emotional response that encourages their decisions. It is likely that humans as a species have a specific course to follow, while individuals have the flexibility of choice.

An individual's free will is expressed in their environment, and the environment is impressed on the individual. Life survives by adapting to its surroundings. This necessity induces a natural response, causing adjustments in an animal's physiology and allowing it to tolerate and then thrive in a changing climate. The farther an animal gets from the equator, the larger its pineal gland. Penguins have the largest pineal gland proportionally, while animals living close to the equator have smaller pineal glands. Crocodiles and edentates (sloths, anteaters, and armadillos) do not have a pineal gland.[2] Natives of northern Siberia have fatty deposits around the eyes and sinuses, creating an oval shape or epicanthic fold around the eye, which helps insulate and protect them from cold temperatures, freezing winds, snow blindness, and UV light.[3] People living closer to the equator have darker complexions to prevent the body from making too much vitamin D, which would calcify in the kidneys and other soft tissues.[4] The dark skin pigment is caused by the production of eumelanin. The farther away from the equator a people group originated, the less eumelanin members of the group produce, and the lighter their skin becomes. Yellow hair is caused by the reduction of eumelanin and the increase in the pigment pheomelanin. Light skin prevents people from developing a vitamin D deficiency in climates that have fewer days of full-spectrum sunlight. Eumelanin has a protective effect against the sun, which makes people with light skin more susceptible to skin cancer than darker-skinned people. Conversely, people with darker skin are more likely to suffer from a vitamin D deficiency when living in colder climates.[5] A person does not choose where they are born or how their body responds to their environment, but individual choices and behavior create specific changes that assist and reflect personal lifestyles and foci.

Unlike plants and animals, people have the power to grow consciously.[6] Once an individual sets their focus on an objective, the pursuit of the goal will cause the body and brain to develop the faculties to obtain it. Dr. Julius Wolff, a respected surgeon in the nineteenth century, noticed that bone, the most rigid and "fixed" aspect of the body, remodels itself based on use. If a particular bone is experiencing persistent stress (from exercise or a vocation), it will become stronger. Likewise, bones that are free from stress will atrophy and become weaker over time. This observation became known as Wolff's law.[7] A bodybuilder has the freedom to overdevelop or underdevelop any body part by adjusting their workouts. This same freedom can be applied to the brain and the skills associated with its different regions. When a person engages in a cognitive task, the blood flow to the brain significantly increases.[8] Elevated blood flow will bring more nutrients and increase the ability to clear metabolic waste products, which allows that area of the body to develop. Moreover, levels of choline, creatine, and sialic acid, chemicals that aid development, will also increase when someone is learning a new concept.[9]

The brain has segregated skills in specific areas. The parietal lobe is responsible for calculating and processing numbers, the frontal lobe is used to recall numerical knowledge and working memory, and Broca's area is linked to speech production.[10] Since the brain is compartmentalized, the individual has the ability to develop specific attributes through focus and practice, much like a bodybuilder chooses what muscles to train. A person has the freedom to develop in the way she or he chooses. However, each person has a specific growth pattern or line that is easiest for them.[11] This is why different people have an innate ability to develop talents and skills at a faster rate than others. Pursuing a career along a natural line of growth will offer less resistance as a person develops their inherent strengths.

Nature will encourage and reward applied conscious self-development and the cumulative effect of decision-making within the limits of the three laws through vitality, a sense of well-being, and the energy to continue the behavior. The most important factors for a long life are a person's attitude, education, health, and wealth. In basic terms, learning is an exercise for the mind that improves mental plasticity, keeps it sharp, and helps maintain a good memory. Continually learning also helps the individual make better decisions while staying relevant in a changing world. People who persistently make good decisions are more likely to cultivate a positive attitude while embracing change. Positive thinking has a direct impact on longevity. Optimistic people are more likely to live to eighty-five than pessimistic people.[12] Having a positive attitude is an effect of believing that the future will be good or things will work out. People determine the future by analyzing the past. A person's history is the result of applied knowledge, education, and experience, expressed in day-to-day decision-making. Optimism is the emotional product from a history of decisions that have yielded beneficial outcomes.

Conversely, pessimism is fear of change and may be a bellwether for disease. Pessimistic men are four times more likely to suffer from coronary heart disease.[13] Any disease will challenge a person's attitude, lower their resolve, interfere with their focus, and increase anxiety. When these symptoms are brought to the workplace, they can be mistaken for character defects rather than poor health. Health problems will have a direct effect on work performance and potentially create high medical costs, making sick people more likely to be poor than healthy people. Longevity is directly related to illness and indirectly related to wealth. A study conducted between 2001 and 2014 found that the gap in life expectancy between the richest 1 percent and poorest 1 percent was 14.6 years for men and 10.1 years for women.[14] In 2018 the average life expectancy in the United States was 78.5 years. The richest men and women live roughly 20 percent and 15 percent longer than the poorest men and women, respectively.

A person's attitude is affected by their health, but it is also a choice. The outlook someone has on life substantially influences their success. The more effort that goes into cultivating a positive attitude, the better an individual's life will become. Success and optimism are cyclical. Optimism is a form of energy free from fear. Any fear or apprehension that someone carries with them into a job will act as a distraction, shunting energy and focus, reducing the likelihood of success. Optimism gives people the confidence to act, pursue risk, and challenge themselves. It is the impetus for and ally to ambition. Conversely, pessimism is a lack of energy and a type of fear. Any job that is done pessimistically is likely to yield shoddy and incomplete work. These polar-opposite attitudes are really expressions of a belief in results.

People feel safe when they can accurately plan or predict the future. A pessimistic attitude implies that the person does not believe the results or the future will be beneficial or successful, and they may intentionally undermine the job to satisfy their belief and to keep them feeling safe. Since optimism is the opposite attitude, it likely results in success. Consistently approaching life with the same attitude will produce a history of similar outcomes. This validates a person's attitude, bolsters their convictions, and affirms their behaviors. To change the outcome of a person's small successes and failures, they must change their behaviors. Behavior is the product of belief, which is the product of thought, and attitude is the expression of all three. Therefore, changing a negative attitude to a positive one requires a change in thought. What a person thinks is a choice, making success a choice.

CHAPTER 2:
THOUGHT AND AUTOSUGGESTION

"Thought is the only power which can produce tangible riches from the Formless Substance. The stuff from which all things are made is a substance which thinks, and a thought of form in this substance produces the form."[15] We are living at the interface between creation and reality. Nature requires us to adapt to the environment (the reality) we live in, while conscious thought simultaneously allows us to create the environment we want to live in (within the laws of nature). Thought is the essential cause of belief, action, and behavior. By controlling thought(s), a person can change their behavior, and by changing behavior, people change their lives.

Behavior is the outward expression of thought. Taking conscious control of how and what someone thinks directly changes behavior, which allows life to become a choice rather than an environmental consequence. Intentionally choosing what to think or focus on can be extremely difficult. Patience and persistence are essential to accomplishing any long-standing change in thought.

Thought is a product of the mind. In his book *Thought-Force in Business and Everyday Life*,[16] William Atkinson distinctly divides the brain in two personified areas, the "active brother" and the "passive brother." The active brother, or the "I am" consciousness, is vigilant, watchful, suspicious, and always on guard, protecting the passive brother from suggestion and external influence. Conversely, the passive brother, or subconscious, is good natured, easygoing, mechanical, apt to believe almost anything, and willing to grant any request made of it. The "I am" consciousness is located in the cerebrum, and the subconscious is located in the cerebellum (the little brain).[17] For a new thought or intention to be accepted, integrated, and translated into behavior, the "I am" consciousness and the subconscious need to work together. To impregnate the subconscious mind with a conscious thought, space and time must be removed from the command or thought.

The "I am" consciousness and the subconscious have an antagonistic relationship; if the aspects of space and time are eliminated, this polarity is diminished. Saying "I want to stop smoking cigarettes next week" gives the subconscious mind both time and space to place obstacles in the way. A phrase or objective must always be formulated as an order in the present tense. For instance, if one wants to stop smoking, the autosuggestion would be "I am a nonsmoker" or "I have no desire to smoke." Since there is no time and space in the phrase, the subconscious is receptive to the intention and will work in concert with the "I am" consciousness. The phrase "I will stop smoking" expresses both time and space (the distance between the present and a point in the future), and therefore the subconscious will work against the suggestion.

Here are some examples of autosuggestion phrases that are free from time and space:

1. I do not drink alcohol.
2. I am wealthy.

3. I am healthy.
4. There is a solution to every problem.
5. I am not anxious.
6. I get to work on time.
7. I eat breakfast every day.
8. I have a clean house.
9. I do not come into work late.
10. I save 10 percent of my income.
11. I live below my means.
12. I have role models close to me.
13. I am a nondrinker.
14. I have a specific amount of money in the bank.
15. I sleep through the night.
16. I have focused energy all day.

The words people use are a lens that focuses the mind, and they become an imprecation or benison over time. When spoken internally or externally, a suggestion may cause a physical response like rejection at first. A strong reaction to a new suggestion by the body and mind is the first sign of change. Autosuggestion is an exercise that focuses the mind.

The ideal times to practice autosuggestion are before going to sleep and after waking up. These two times of day are when the brain is theta wave dominant. The reduction of alpha waves and increase in theta waves cause sleepiness. Theta waves are produced in the hippocampus, which is responsible for learning, memory (short and long term), and spatial navigation. The hippocampus is also where new neurons are made (adult neurogenesis). Practicing autosuggestion while the brain is theta wave dominant is likely to target the hippocampus more effectively than when other brain waves are dominant, which will increase the ability to program new neurons. The new neurons, like children, are pliable and more receptive to suggestion and are therefore able to be internalized and be expressed as the suggestion. Moreover, practicing autosuggestion during theta-dominant brain activity may directly affect the mature cells of the brain and body and effectively reshape one's identity according to one's will. Identity is self-reflection through experience and memory. Autosuggestion effectively reassociates memories and experiences, as it shapes the mind to the will of the individual so that they can create their chosen identity.

"Try saying "war" or "cancer" or "money" ten thousand times, and you will find that your whole mood has been changed and colored by the association connected with that word."[18] By persistently repeating an intention, the individual begins to express this desire as a core aspect of their behavior. If the suggestion were "I am a focused thinker," the person over time would take on traits of a focused thinker. To accomplish this or any other suggestion, the consciousness will intentionally begin to change the person's lifestyle to produce the condition of the suggestion, in this case, that of a focused thinker. Changes in lifestyle will come as natural urges that begin faintly at first and gradually build into strong desires. In this example, the person may have a desire to eat differently, meditate, and research techniques to improve focus. If the intention were "I am rich," these desires may center on investment research, finding a mentor, getting a higher-paying job, learning a more "valuable" skill, or finding ways to lower monthly spending. Autosuggestion is an inculcated exercise that demands persistence and patience. The fulfillment of a desire through autosuggestion is realized through nature. The individual grows into the reality of the autosuggestion. The process takes time.

"Not one-fourth of our thoughts are our own, but are simply picked up from the atmosphere."[19] The community we live in, coworkers, family members, friends, television programs, and music all play a dynamic role in what we think and what we value. Therefore, finding time to be alone and reflective is ideal for choosing a life specific to the individual. During each reflective session, write down a list of desires and date it. After a month of doing this, compare the first and last day's lists. As focus turns inward, the individual releases external influences, which give way to personal desires. Redirecting consciousness in this way will cause changes in the person's list of desires over time.

Autosuggestion Summary

1. Write a list of desires each day for a month; date and save them (this will help connect you to your true desires).
2. Repeat the desire(s) as a mantra free from time and space. "I earn $100K a year," not "I *will* earn $100K a year." The word *will* (a future tense) implies that you do not earn $100K a year.
3. Practice autosuggestion at night before going to sleep and when first waking up. Autosuggestion is effective when practiced anytime; however, these times are specifically effective.
4. Be persistent and patient.
5. As urges to change your behavior grow, act on them.
6. Periodically review older desires (over the months or years) to evaluate the results.

CHAPTER 3:

ELECTROMAGNETIC WAVES AND TELEPATHY

On June 3, 1880, Alexander Graham Bell and Charles Sumner Tainter invented the photophone using electromagnetic waves. It was a device that transmitted the first wireless spoken message using sunlight as an electromagnetic carrier. The photophone worked by projecting a voice through an instrument toward a mirror. The vibrations of the voice caused the mirror to oscillate in harmony with the vibrations of the voice. Alexander then directed sunlight onto the mirror, which captured and projected the oscillating patterns toward another mirror, where the oscillating patterns were transformed back into sound at the receiving end of the projection.

Humans have adapted to the electromagnetic energy of sunlight. The pineal gland stops synthesizing melatonin when the body is exposed to sunlight. Sunlight can lower blood pressure by releasing nitric oxide from the skin into the circulatory system. UV rays from the sun catalyze the synthesis of vitamin D by converting 7-dehydrocholesterol in the skin to cholecalciferol, a precursor to the active form of vitamin

D. Humans and animals also unknowingly react to the man-made electromagnetic fields ubiquitous today. High-voltage power lines, antitheft systems, metal detectors, batteries, digital watches, cameras, flashlights, televisions, automatic garage door openers, cell phones, and kitchen appliances release various types of magnetic fields. Weak electromagnetic fields common in business settings raise acetylcholine levels in the brain stem, which act as a subliminal distress signal for the body without our conscious awareness. Rats release the stress hormone cortisol when exposed to microwaves. Prolonged exposure to microwaves exhausts the rat's adrenal cortex and causes depression.[20] Living organisms are directly affected by the electromagnetic fields in their environment. Moreover, some animals have become reliant on them as a means for orientation and communication.

The ability to detect delicate changes in the local electromagnetic field allows birds and marine animals to establish migration patterns, avoid predators, hunt prey, communicate, and find a mate. Marine animals' electromagnetic sense has evolved multiple times across many taxa, indicating the persistence and utility of electromagnetic fields for animals.[21] It is possible to perceive electromagnetic fields via magnetite and cryptochrome. Magnetite, a permanent magnetic form of iron oxide, is found in the noses and beaks of many fish and birds. The mineral contains equal amounts of iron(II) and iron(III) and has the empirical formula Fe_3O_4. It is commonly found in igneous, metamorphic, and sedimentary rocks. Magnetite is extremely sensitive to magnetic fields, giving it the ability to act as a compass and orientation tool for migratory animals. Cryptochromes are photoreceptors found in fish, insects, amphibians, plants, and mammals that regulate circadian rhythms by reacting to light. Cryptochromes are a type of flavoprotein (protein bound with a nucleic acid derivative) found in the retinas of many mammals. When blue or ultraviolet light strikes a cryptochrome protein, the energy changes the protein's electron structure, giving it the ability to react to electromagnetic fields.[22]

Magnetite and cryptochrome are found in humans. The breakdown of ferritin and bacteria that produce the magnetite crystal (commonly found in animals known to use magnetic fields) are the leading hypothesis as to how it ends up in the brain. In humans, magnetite crystals are found in the pineal gland, sphenoid and ethmoid bones (bridge of the nose), cerebellum, brain stem, and left hemisphere of the brain.[23] Humans have two genes that code for cryptochrome, CRY1 and CRY2. Both are expressed in the retina and pineal gland.[24] Magnetite and cryptochrome contribute to the brain's sensitivity to changing electromagnetic fields.

The body and brain's sensitivity to electromagnetic fields implies that they are sensitive to patterns in electromagnetic fields as well. A pattern in an electromagnetic field is information. Guglielmo Marconi laid the groundwork for humans to send audio messages over long distances by inventing the wireless radio which created specific patterns in electromagnetic fields that a receiving device can translate back into a facsimile of the original message. For humans to telepathically communicate with each other through electromagnetic fields, the body and brain would require the same capacity.

Magnetite and cryptochrome provide the body and brain with their sensitivity and awareness to external electromagnetic fields. The body's pH and ability to store and move electrons create the potential to produce electromagnetic waves that carry thought. Electromagnetic waves were discovered by Hans Christian Oersted, André-Marie Ampère, and others in the early nineteenth century. James Clerk Maxwell (1831–1879) developed four equations stating that an electric current produces an electric and magnetic wave. Electric and magnetic waves are continuous, can travel through space, carry information, and never end.[25] An electric current is a stream of charged particles (electrons) moving through space or along a surface.

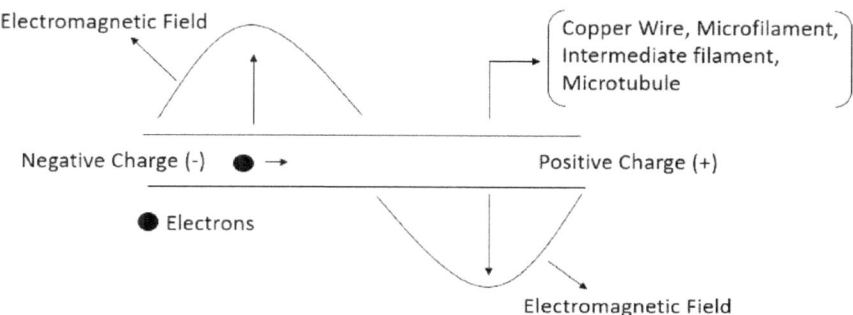

Dr. Jerry Tennant claims the body stores electrons in the cells' membranes. When a cell is damaged or dividing, it raises the electric potential fifty millivolts so that it can heal and divide correctly.[26] The cell does this by releasing stored electrons from the membrane through the cytoskeleton. The cytoskeleton comprises three different types of protein: microfilaments, intermediate filaments, and microtubules. Microfilaments are thin, threadlike proteins made from actin. Intermediate filaments have a larger diameter than microfilaments; they are made of several strands of fibrous proteins wound together. Microtubules are small, hollow tubes made of the proteins α-tubulin and β-tubulin.[27]

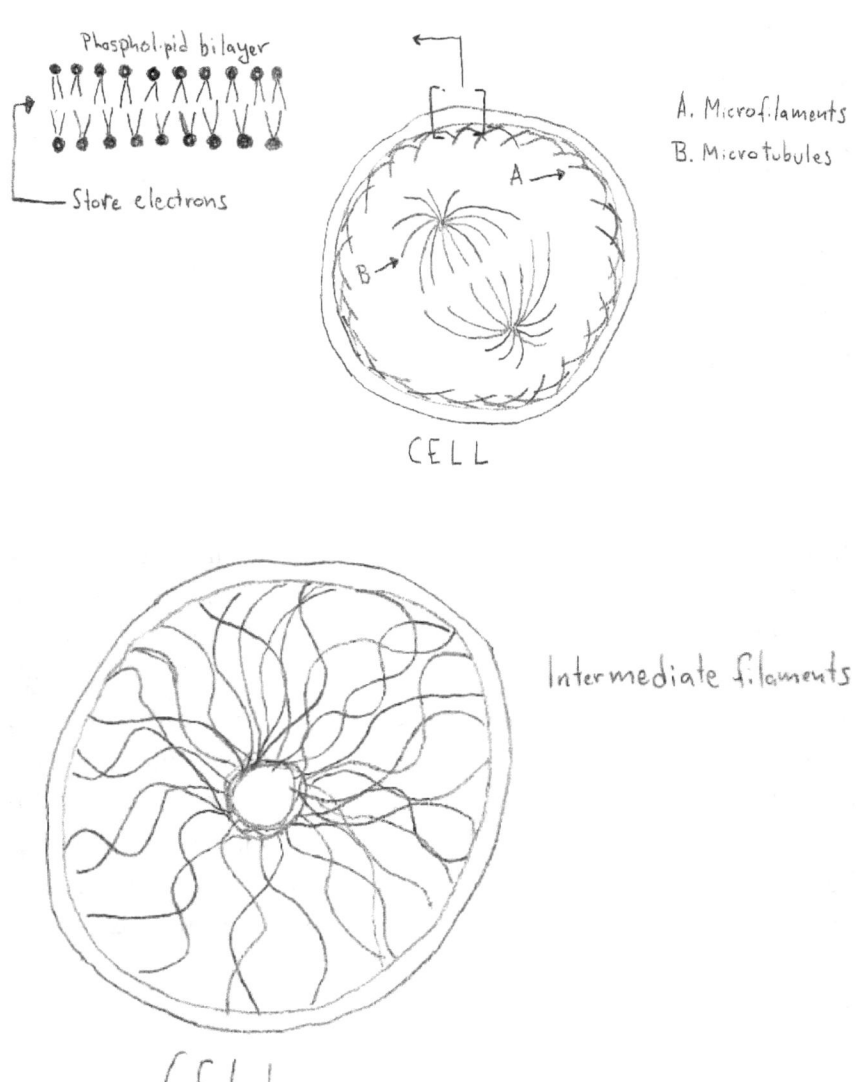

As the electrons move into the cell through the cytoskeleton, they create an electric current. The electric current in turn creates an electromagnetic wave capable of sending information to other cells in the body and into the environment.

There are roughly thirty trillion cells in the human body. Practicing autosuggestion on a continuous basis allows more cells to harmonize with a person's objectives while they project their thoughts into the environment. Animals of different shapes distort or interact with electromagnetic fields differently.[28] When a person crystalizes their objectives through repetition and focus, it creates a defined shape in the electromagnetic field that may specifically influence one's circumstances and the individuals related to that particular thought (or message). The dominating thought will also organize cells internally to influence the behavioral changes needed to acquire one's objectives.

Samael Aun Weor, a respected occultist and spiritual leader, claimed in his book *The Perfect Matrimony*, originally published in 1950, that the body and brain transmit and receive thoughts from other people:

"The third center is the church of Pergamos. This is the brain of Emotions. We have established within the human organism a veritable wireless station. The receiver is the umbilical center. The transmitting antenna is the pineal gland. Mind waves of those who think about us reach the umbilical center, or the brain of emotion, and later pass to the brain where we become consciously aware of these thoughts."[29]

The brain of the emotions likely refers to the enteric nervous system, found in the gut. The church of Pergamos is the chakra near the navel, also called the svadhisthana sacral chakra in yogic anatomy. Chakras are located where major nerves branch along the spine. Nerve cells directly align themselves to external currents and electromagnetic fields. Moreover, the nervous system associated with the spinal cord is positive in relation to the nerves in the extremities (the polarities flip at night), which suggests that external electromagnetic energy is more likely to enter the body at these positive centers, the same way electrons move toward the positive end of a battery.[30] The pineal gland acts as a transmitting antenna, supporting the hypothesis that sending and receiving thoughts through an electromagnetic field is the basis of telepathy. Modern science has proved that the magnetite and cryptochrome in the pineal gland are capable of sensing and influencing electromagnetic fields, giving credibility to the proclamation made by Samael Aun Weor.

Electrons are required for an individual to effectively project telepathic thoughts and unify the cells of the body with the will of the mind. The body acquires electrons from ionic transfers, moving water, unprocessed food, celibacy, and exercise.[31] When the body touches something or someone with more electrons than itself, some of the electrons will be transferred to that body. Hugging and grounding are common forms of ionic transfer. Muscle and bone act as rechargeable batteries.[32] When they expand and contract during exercise, they generate electrons, making them piezoelectric (able to release an electric charge under physical stress).[33]

Food directly influences blood pH; pH determines whether a solution is acidic or basic. Acidic solutions take electrons. Basic solutions donate them. A pH below 7 is acidic. A pH above 7 is alkaline A healthy blood pH is 7.4. Blood with a pH of 7.4 can donate electrons to cells when they are needed, ensuring that the cells have the current necessary to remain healthy. A person has four to six liters of blood, which is pumped through the circulatory system at seventy-five milliliters per heartbeat, or 5.25 liters per minute.[34] The circulatory system is a closed circuit and a type of connective tissue that has direct contact with all cells in the body. A blood pH of 7.4 has an electric charge of minus-twenty millivolts.[35] As basic blood moves through the circulatory system, it creates an electric current. As an electric current, blood adopts the role of a carrier wave, transferring thoughts from cell to cell throughout the body. Blood also produces an electromagnetic wave that can project thoughts into the environment.

The pH of blood slowly becomes acidic as the body ages. Acidic blood with a pH below 7 is no longer able to donate electrons to cells as they need them, which impairs the cells' capacity to communicate with one another. People who have acidic blood take or steal electrons from the environment and lose their telepathic mechanism, resulting in a diminished ability to influence others. Individuals who subconsciously prefer healthy, high-energy environments may naturally avoid people with acidic blood and places that steal electrons.

Food directly affects the pH of blood. The stomach releases hydrochloric acid from the parietal cells to break down dietary protein. Sodium bicarbonate is made and released into the blood at the same time. This process is known as "alkaline tide" because sodium bicarbonate raises the pH or alkalinity of the circulatory system. Stomach cells require a balanced intake of protein, calcium, iron, magnesium, phosphorus, sodium, chloride, potassium, vitamin B1, iodine, zinc, carbon dioxide, and water to make hydrochloric acid and sodium bicarbonate.[36]

Edgar Cayce was famously known as the "sleeping prophet" and "father of holistic medicine" during the early 1900s. He explained the importance of maintaining a proper alkaline and acid balance for optimum health. In his book *Edgar Cayce on Healing Foods for Body, Mind, and Soul*, William A. McGarey outlines Cayce's food recommendations and the importance of eating 80 percent alkaline foods and 20 percent acidic foods.[37] McGarey recommends choosing foods from the following options:

Alkaline-Forming Foods:

Vegetables: artichokes, asparagus, beans, beets, cabbage, carob, carrots, cauliflower, celery, eggplant, endives, green peas, kale, lettuce, mushrooms, mustard greens, okra, onions (white), oyster plants, parsley, parsnips, peppers (green), poke greens, potatoes (sweet), potatoes (white), radishes, rutabaga, salsify, spinach, sprouts, string beans, tomatoes, turnips, watercress

Fruit: apples (eaten alone), apricots, bananas, berries (except cranberries), dates, figs, grapes, grapefruit, guava, limes, melons, oranges, papaya, peaches, pears, pineapples, pomegranates, prunes, quinces, raisins, most other fruits

Milk and milk products: buttermilk, cream, milk, yogurt

Miscellaneous alkaline: desserts such as ice cream and Jell-O, lentils, oils (olive and peanut), pumpernickel, honey

Acid-Forming Foods:

Grains and their products: bread (corn, sourdough, rye, whole wheat; toasted is best), cereals (especially cooked steel-cut oats, cracked wheat, wheat and barley, corn rice, wheat germ), crackers, pancakes (whole wheat, buckwheat, corn, rice), rice

Meats: fish (baked, boiled, broiled, etc.; never fried), seafood of all kinds, beef, lamb, poultry, wild game

Miscellaneous acids: beef juice, butter, cakes, cookies, pastries, cheese (cheddar and cottage), corn (sweet), cranberries, eggs (yolk preferred), margarine, nuts (almonds, filberts; near neutral: peanuts, English walnuts, Brazil nuts)

Meditation

Dr. Cleve Backster accidentally discovered that plants are telepathic by using a lie detector machine. He placed the electrodes of the machine on a houseplant (*Dracaena massangeana*) and thought about burning it. The lie detector machine recorded a strong reaction by the plant at the moment Backster thought about burning it. This event led Backster to a lifetime of experiments using the lie detector machine on plants, sperm, and other living organisms. He concluded in part that plants have memory; are sentient, telepathic, and emotional; and form attachments with people over long distances. Backster also speculated from his experiments that this telepathic communication is a subtle perception that is largely washed out by the five human senses (touch, sight, smell, taste, hearing).[38]

Backster provided evidence that thoughts affect others and the environment even if they are not acted on, implying that they are governed by the law of karma. Karma is the most exalted and irrefutable law, summarized by the maxim "For whatsoever a man sowest, that shall he also reap."[39] Therefore, positive thoughts and negative thoughts have corresponding consequences. Telepathy increases the importance of autosuggestion. As individuals reprogram themselves, they are also broadcasting their intentions to the world. The subtle function of telepathy is likely behind life's serendipity and the urge that drives men and women to action.

Sunlight is both an electromagnetic wave and a particle. This suggests that thoughts are individual particles that release or produce electromagnetic waves specific to that thought. Swami Sivananda claimed that every thought has weight, shape, size, form, color, quality, and power.[40] A person's identity becomes tangled in their dominating thoughts, which cause false self-perceptions. Meditation allows the person to detangle thoughts from their consciousness and witness them objectively. Meditation is an exercise that is developed through repetition and carries a profound list of benefits that include the separation of thought and consciousness. By separating their thoughts from their consciousness, a person is able to understand that they are not the thought. This allows them to take control of what they think and reestablish a more accurate self-perception. Meditation also causes the individual to withdraw from their five senses. Absorption in the five senses is likely one of the reasons people are unaware of their natural, subtle telepathic sense. Meditation increases a person's awareness and helps to detangle the consciousness from dominating thoughts so that the individual can objectively witness them.

Benefits of Meditation

Lowers cortisol	Lowers adrenaline	Improves asthma symptoms	Improves psoriasis	Lowers depression
Lowers stress	Increases melatonin	Increases immune system activity	Lowers heart rate	Lowers blood pressure
Improves focus	Improves stress-related IBS	Increases DHEA	Boosts energy	Increases self-acceptance
Fewer behavioral outbursts	Releases negative thoughts	Lowers drug and alcohol abuse	Reduces pain	Increases HGH
Increases awareness	Increases intuition			

Meditation has the capacity to profoundly change an individual's life. Meditation is ideally preceded by light stretching and a few minutes of pranayama. The fifteen-minute warm-up exercise series in the book *Transitions to a Heart-Centered World* by Yogi Bjahan increases the flexibility of the spine and lengthens the muscles in the legs, which will allow the individual to sit in comfort longer.[41]

Warm-Up Exercise Set:

1. Camel ride: Sitting on your heels (rock pose), flex the spine back and forth, inhaling when the stomach is out and exhaling when it is tucked in. Repeat for two to three minutes.
2. Twist: In rock pose, with your hands on your shoulders (hands in front and thumbs in back) and a straight spine, inhale and turn to the left, and exhale and turn to the right. Repeat for two to three minutes.
3. Shoulder shrug: With your hands on your knees in rock pose, inhale, raising your shoulders to your ears, and exhale as they fall. Repeat for two to three minutes.
4. Neck rolls: In rock pose with your hands on your knees, place your chin on your chest, slowly circle your head to the right (so your right ear reaches toward your right shoulder), then across the back and to the left side (so your left ear reaches toward your left shoulder). Return your chin to your chest. Repeat for two to three minutes in each direction. Inhale while the head is moving across the back, and exhale while the head is moving across the front.
5. Cat-cow: On hands and knees (hands shoulder width apart, knees hip width apart), arch your back up on the exhale and lower your head to your chest. On the inhale, let your stomach fall to the floor while raising your head up. The stomach and lower back drive the motion with the shoulders; the head

follows the motion. When the motion becomes comfortable, the speed can be increased. Repeat for two to three minutes.

6. A. Life nerve stretch: Sitting with both legs straight out in front of you, grab your toes by bending at the hips, and slowly pull the head down toward the knees while exhaling. Remain in position, moving only to adjust for breathing, for one to two minutes. B. Place your left heel on the inside of your right thigh, and repeat the exercise described in 6a. Then place your right heel on the inside of your left thigh. Repeat for one to two minutes for each leg.
7. While seated, spread your legs out wide apart, rotate your torso square over one leg, bend from your hips, and grab your toes on the exhale. On the inhale, rise up, twist your torso over the opposite leg, exhale, bend from the hips, and grab your toes. Repeat for one to two minutes.

Pranayama

Pranayama is the practice of controlling the breath, or breathing exercises. There are hundreds of different pranayamas, or breathing exercises, with varying benefits and purposes. Nadi shodhana, or alternate nostril breathing, is the most revered and important pranayama in yoga. Nadi is an energy channel, and shodhana is cleansing or purifying. Nadi shodhana is cleansing or purifying the energy channels. Nadi shodhana is a complete practice and is considered a panacea because it balances the autonomic nervous system.

Mudra, or Hand Position, for Nadi Shodhana:
Place the right hand over the face. Place the tips of the index and middle fingers gently on the eyebrow center. Both fingers should be relaxed. Hold the thumb just above the right nostril and the ring finger just above the left nostril. The thumb and ring finger control the flow

of the breath in the nostrils. Alternately press one nostril, blocking the flow of breath, then release and press the other.

Sit in a comfortable position with a straight spine.

Follow these steps for one complete cycle of nadi shodhana:
1. Close the right nostril with the right thumb and inhale through the left nostril.
2. Hold the inhale.
3. Close the left nostril with the right ring finger, and exhale through the right nostril.
4. Hold the exhale.
5. Inhale through the right nostril with the left nostril closed.
6. Hold the inhale.
7. Close the right nostril with the right thumb and exhale through the left nostril.
8. Hold the exhale.

Inhale and exhale for equal amounts of time. The inhales and exhales should be of equal lengths to avoid light-headedness.

This is one complete cycle of nadi shodhana. It is important to practice this exercise in complete cycles. The effects of nadi shodhana can be experienced in as little as three minutes.

Benefits of Nadi Shodhana:[42]
- Inhaling through one nostril stimulates the opposite brain hemisphere. Nadi shodhana balances both brain hemispheres.
- Stimulates and relaxes the autonomic nervous system.
- Stimulates the sympathetic nervous system when inhaling through the right nostril.
- Stimulates the parasympathetic nervous system when inhaling through the left nostril.
- Activates the frontal brain, inducing tranquility, clarity of thought, and concentration.

- Maintains the pineal gland and balances the endocrine system.
- Helps remove depressive tendencies.

Set an alarm clock before meditation. This allows you to sink further into meditation without being concerned about time.

Sit with a straight spine in a comfortable position free from distractions. Close the eyes or slightly turn them inward toward the bridge of the nose, rest the hands comfortably on the knees or lap, and focus on the breath. Breathe naturally through the nose; when thoughts come up, gently return the focus back to the breath. Mindful meditation helps withdraw the consciousness from the senses and separate the mind from thought, creating a state of deep relaxation.

Sleep

People who meditate regularly tend to need less sleep than people who don't. In both states the "I am" consciousness withdraws from the five senses, creating an increased dialogue with the subconscious. Communication between the "I am" consciousness and the subconscious is essential for self-fulfillment and connecting with the world. Self-fulfillment as an organism means survival. Survival is a program hardwired into life. Animals will do nearly anything to survive. Reproduction is an expression of survival because it allows the organism to pass on its genes, memories, and legacy. The urge to bear children is the urge to survive. The body is communicating with the world and with others in ways the "I am" consciousness is not aware of, making the body telepathic.

The "I am" consciousness withdraws during sleep, which may allow telepathic communication to become more active as energy is shunted into different parts of the body. When the "I am" consciousness sleeps, the subconscious is most active, operating through the reproductive center. Since sex is an expression of survival, nocturnal penile and clitoral tumescence could indicate that the body is reaching out in search of a mate telepathically. The idea of nocturnal sexual telepathy may explain the personification of the succubus and incubus. Moreover, it implies that the subconscious is actively influencing the decisions people make. Many people presume that the subconscious is merely a receptive faculty for the impressions of the "I am" consciousness, but the urge to mate and other animal instincts are clear evidence that the subconscious is an active influence in life.

Many view telepathy as a supernatural power. Supernatural powers are manufactured in the sexual center.[43] Mystical powers, like telepathy and precognition, are likely inherent functions of the body and nature operating in the electromagnetic field. In his book *Initiation into Hermetics*, Franz Bardon illustrates that each body part is subdivided into electric and magnetic components. To keep the illustration germane, the reproductive areas are described here. The male genitals are divided as follows: The front part is electric, the back part is neutral, and the right and left sides are neutral. The inside is magnetic. The female genitals are divided as follows: The back part is neutral, and the right and left sides are neutral. The inside is electric.[44] Bardon and Dr. Jerry Tennent have concluded through separate channels that the body is electromagnetic in nature and thereby able to communicate telepathically. Swami Vivekananda also supports this conjecture while localizing the telepathic faculty to the reproductive center; in doing so, he emphasizes the importance of sleep. While the body sleeps, the sexual center is active and therefore telepathic.

Presuming that nocturnal sexual ideation is a warped interpretation of active subconscious telepathy searching to reproduce for survival implies that the subconscious can be used by the "I am" consciousness to telepathically draw out other intended opportunities. Consciously repeating intentions or suggestions (without referring to time and space) while falling asleep may influence the subconscious to scan the environment during sleep, "looking" to fulfill the intention.

If someone's intention was "I am a movie star," then the subconscious would locate an acting studio, agent, or whatever that person required to become a movie star. Answers that come to people while they sleep are the subconscious fulfillment of the request of the "I am" consciousness. The perception of precognition is the subconscious relaying information to the "I am" consciousness. The subconscious has already communicated with the person who will give the future movie star their first "big break" and is relaying this to the "I am" consciousness as a feeling or sense that an opportunity is coming. Proper sleep is likely to increase the connection between the "I am" consciousness and the subconscious, making it invaluable in the pursuit of self-fulfillment.

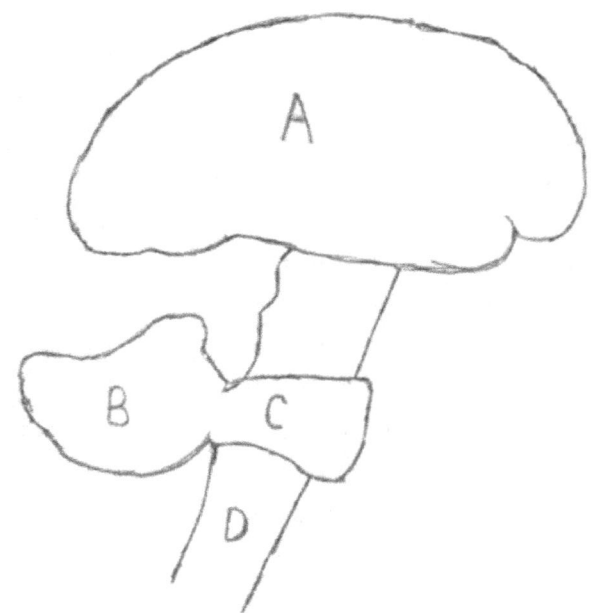

A. Cerebrum **B.** Cerebellum **C.** Pons **D.** Spinal cord

Support for sleep as a medium to connect the subconscious with the "I am" consciousness comes from the process itself. Dreams are generated from the pontine brain stem (pons or pons Varolii), releasing electrical energy during REM sleep. The electrical energy from the pons emanates out from the brain stem toward the midbrain and cerebrum. "Pons" is Latin for "bridge" and is possibly used as the name for this portion of the brain because it connects the cerebellum, or little brain (subconscious), to the cerebrum (normal or "I am" consciousness) by way of the midbrain. The subconscious may use the pons as a projector to send messages to the cerebrum.

Sleep is a physiological, mechanical process with defined time intervals and characteristics. The trigger, power supply, clock, and dream state generator for sleep are all located in the pons.[45] Since sleep is a repeating, predictable process, it is implied that the electrical energy used to generate dreams is also predictable and therefore patterned. Patterned energy is information, which means that the brain stem is projecting information out toward the cerebrum. Dreams may seem random or unrelatable because of a language disconnect between the brain stem, cerebellum, and cerebrum. The brain stem and cerebellum likely function with a different type of sensory awareness than the cerebrum. If so, this would cause the cerebellum to form independent relationships and associations with the rest of the body and environment. The electrical energy generated from the pons that is used to produce dreams is sent in patterns relevant to the language of the cerebellum, not the language of the cerebrum.

Stearn Robinson and Tom Corbett worked together to write *The Dreamer's Dictionary*, which illustrates how objects and scenarios that happen in dreams have different meanings to the subconscious and waking consciousness.[46] Examples offered in the book include the following:

Menu: A dream which features a menu promises a long period of comfortable if not luxurious living.

Gorilla: To dream of this big ape portends a painful misunderstanding, unless the animal was very docile or definitely friendly, in which case the dream forecasts a very unusual new friend.

Feces: All sources pretty well agree that excrement (whether human or animal) in a dream represents money, wealth, profits or tangible value and is a lucky omen pertaining to material gain. See also *bowel movement*.

Scissors: Scissors, as such, featured in a dream are thought to portend a broken relationship; but to use scissors signifies that you can outwit a jealous competitor by prompt action.

Pecans: You can expect an advantageous social invitation if you dreamed of eating pecans. See also *nuts* and *trees*.

Moss: If the moss in your dream was dry and/or discolored, it portends disenchantment; but if it was soft and green, it predicts romantic bliss.

The body and brain require sleep to stay healthy, and for that reason sleep is needed for success. Sleep produces an anabolic state that repairs and restores the immune, nervous, skeletal, and muscular systems. The brain specifically needs sleep to function properly. The glymphatic system is particularly active during sleep, removing metabolic waste from the brain. Glycogen, the brain's fuel, is restored, and a person's mood, cognitive function, and memory are maintained. The benefits from sleep are due in part to the increased production of melatonin, testosterone, and growth hormone as well as the increase in theta and delta waves. Melatonin, lauded as an antiaging hormone, has antioxidant properties, maintains circadian rhythms, regulates sexual development, and acts as an anti-inflammatory chemical for the immune system. Growth hormone is an anabolic hormone that stimulates growth, cell reproduction, and cell regeneration. Theta waves are most prevalent just before sleep and just after waking up. They are essential for learning, storing memories, and spatial navigation. It is when the brain is theta dominant that an individual can internalize their desire(s), which helps to realign the person's focus to accomplish their goals. Theta waves do this by increasing the dialogue between the "I am" consciousness and the subconscious. Delta waves are most prevalent during sleep. Delta waves stimulate the release of growth hormone and prolactin, another anabolic hormone. They are the dominant brain waves of infants and begin to diminish during adolescence. They can be completely absent at later stages in life. Children are forced to adapt to their environment, while elderly people are commonly labeled as rigid thinkers or "set in their ways." Mental plasticity can thus be attributed to delta waves. Mental plasticity is essential for growth and development, two characteristics associated with success. To move from a condition of poverty to a life of security and comfort demands personal redefinition and environmental reassociation, which are unachievable without mental plasticity.

A healthy night's sleep depends on a person's diet and lifestyle. Balancing neurotransmitter levels, especially serotonin and dopamine, is essential for proper thinking and healthy sleep. High dopamine levels and low serotonin levels can interfere with sleep. Serotonin and dopamine tend to have an inverse relationship. When serotonin levels go up, dopamine levels go down, and vice versa. Serotonin is used to make melatonin, which in turn regulates the body's sleep-wake cycles. The body produces most of its melatonin at night, creating vanishingly small amounts during the day. Therefore, increasing serotonin production should increase melatonin levels and help maintain a proper sleep cycle. Low serotonin levels can cause depression, chronic fatigue, insomnia, and anger. High dopamine levels can cause elevated libido, anxiety, psychosis, increased energy, mania, heightened focus, and difficulty sleeping.

Even though dopamine and serotonin are endogenous chemicals, the body needs vitamins and minerals from food to make them. To make serotonin from the amino acid tryptophan, the body needs folate, calcium, iron, vitamin B3, zinc, vitamin B6, magnesium, and vitamin C. To make dopamine from the amino acids phenylalanine and tyrosine, the body needs folate, iron, zinc, copper, magnesium, niacin (B3), vitamin B6, and vitamin C. Other than calcium and copper, the core vitamins and minerals used to make dopamine and serotonin are the same. Imbalances between these neurotransmitters and the vitamins and minerals that are needed to synthesize them can develop through diet and lifestyle choices. Addictive behavior is caused by spiking dopamine levels. Coffee, alcohol, gambling, marijuana, and most stimulants raise dopamine levels. High-protein and low-carbohydrate diets and several bodybuilding supplements are also known to raise dopamine levels. Conversely, serotonin levels are increased by carbohydrates, tryptophan, methionine, SAMe, 5-HTP, melatonin, inositol, and vitamin D. Exercise and probiotics can affect both serotonin and dopamine activity. A healthy diet and lifestyle will harmonize the ebb and flow between dopamine and serotonin, providing restorative sleep at night and focused energy during the day.

The Stark Contrast between Restful, Restorative Sleep and Persistent Insomnia

Benefits of sleep:
- Maintains a healthy weight.
- Reduces stress.
- Lowers chance of diabetes.
- Lowers chance of heart disease.
- Increases optimism.
- Increases problem-solving skills.
- Improves self-esteem.
- Clearer thinking.
- Get along better with people.
- Get sick less often.
- Recover from illness more quickly.

Results of insomnia:
- Increases chance of stomach ulcers.
- Lowers neuron production.
- Impairs decision-making.
- Increases the stress hormone corticosterone.
- Decreases growth hormone production.
- Increases anxiety.
- Impairs ability to learn new things.
- Increases chances of cancer.
- Increases chances of depression.
- Can lead to psychosis.

Establishing a nighttime routine will help train the mind and body to prepare for sleep. Listed below are some recommendations to help you fall asleep.

1. Remove all electronics from the bedroom other than an alarm clock.
2. Be in bed a half hour before falling asleep.
3. Wear glasses with orange lenses at night. Orange glasses help maintain natural circadian rhythms by blocking blue light.
4. Use orange or red night-lights and alarm clocks.
5. Go to bed and wake up at the same time every day.
6. Sleep in a completely dark room.
7. Keep the room's temperature below 70 degrees Fahrenheit.
8. Do not go to bed angry or mentally disturbed.
9. Take a hot shower if needed for relaxation and to help with insomnia.
10. Practice meditation or a breathing exercise. Lightly breathing through the left nostril has a calming effect and helps produce theta and delta waves by activating the right brain hemisphere.
11. Lie down on your right side with a pillow between your legs. This position closes the right nostril while opening the left, increasing the production of theta and delta waves.
12. Fall asleep to a positive mantra, aphorism, or intention. The mantra "I am falling asleep" can be used if you are suffering from insomnia.
13. Avoid serious topics, loud music, or television programs before bed.
14. Read before bed.
15. Exercise in the morning or early afternoon.

Restful natural sleep is a process of repairing, rebuilding, and detoxing the body and brain. Answers to lingering problems and optimistic changes in perspective are developed during proper sleep. Healthy sleep is a succor for establishing a sense of direction because it helps you process and externalize deeper goals and desires. Higher forms of communication are conducted within and outside the body during sleep; this creates the security, self-awareness, and confidence to pursue personal ambitions.

CHAPTER 4:
STRESS AND FEAR

Insomnia shares many symptoms with chronic stress. Persistent lack of sleep can cause elevation of the stress hormone corticosterone. Corticosterone and the stress hormone cortisol can cause serious problems for the body and brain. The brain can experience structural and functional changes from prolonged elevated levels of cortisol. Memory and cortisol have an inverse relationship; when cortisol goes up, memory goes down, and vice versa. Short- and long-term memory, along with declarative memory (a type of long-term memory that retrieves facts and events) and spatial memory, are negatively affected by continual stress. People who are constantly subjected to stress can develop cognitive, mood, and memory disorders and exhibit behavior similar to clinical depression. The functional changes of declining memory and impaired cognitive faculties reflect the physical changes incurred from chronic stress. The hippocampus is specifically affected by persistent elevated levels of cortisol. Cells of the hippocampus begin to die, and the ability to produce new neurons is shut down. This leads to atrophy in the hippocampus and other parts of the brain, causing the brain to lose mass and weight.

Several other hormones and molecules that affect the gut, cardiovascular system, and immune system are released because of stress. People are more likely to suffer from a disease after a sudden, major, or extremely stressful lifestyle change. A person who suffers from persistent stress is also more likely to suffer from frequent illness and develop cancer. High blood pressure, blood clotting disorders, and arterial plaque formation are more commonly found in people who suffer from severe stress. Inflammation of the intestinal tract and peptic ulcers, along with colitis, Crohn's, and IBS, are negatively affected by chronic stress. Childhood stress can accelerate cognitive decline and lead to various diseases as an adult. Extreme mental stress can directly lead to sudden death.

Chronic stress will slowly destroy the body and brain, but short-term stress is beneficial. Short-term stress and stress without an emotional connection can improve memory and sharpen the mind. Preparing to take a test or learning something new improves brain function and plasticity. Under these conditions stress is a form of exercise and does not raise cortisol levels the way chronic emotional stress does.[47]

Chronic emotional stress specifically damages the hippocampus, the area of the brain that is more receptive to theta waves and autosuggestion. This affects a person's ability to set new intentions. Since the intentions people set for themselves are waypoints for their future, chronic stress will diminish forward thinking, and proactive decision-making will slowly be replaced by reactive behavior. The physical damage and disconnection between regions of the brain are functionally expressed as memory impairment and other cognitive erosions. This makes problem-solving and learning new concepts more challenging because new concepts and new information are integrated and associated with previously learned concepts. By directly damaging the hippocampus, unhealthy stress limits a person's ability to learn new material and lowers their ability to voluntarily shape their lives. Moreover, forward-looking intentions will be perceived as added stress, making the individual fear the future.

Chronic stress is emotional stress. When someone is chronically stressed, any change will seem overwhelming. Moreover, any unexpected problem will have the potential of causing the person to completely shut down. Not only does stress shrink the brain, but it also shunts blood away from the frontal lobe, the executive decision-making area of the brain. Most problems in life require complex decision-making skills rather than the fight-or-flight response, which is chemically similar to emotional stress. By working together, humans have pulled themselves from the veld to a civilized society. The fight-or-flight response that once helped ensure the survival of the species has become a vestigial echo in animal physiology. Success in today's world requires pragmatic thinking, not the fear-driven, high-stress reaction that our ancestors needed to avoid danger. What threatens a person's well-being has changed. People need to develop a new default response to overcome the problems they face today and leave emotional fear in the past.

People are creatures of habit. Responding to problems with fear is a behavior that has lost value. Emotional stress varies in intensity. Finding and capitalizing on moments of clarity is critical for changing behavior to solve the problems that cause fear. The mind can spend significant time regretting the past and worrying about the future. Accepting fallibility, reconciling past actions, and calculating responses to potential outcomes are all one can do when living outside the moment. At any given time, the most someone can do is make the "best" decision with the information available. Approaching problems this way develops faith in action and a clear conscience.

Unhealthy lifestyles can change someone's chemistry to mimic a fear response. When this happens, a person can project their anxiety into the environment and falsely blame external circumstances as the cause of their stress. Chronic emotional stress is more likely the result of dietary deficiencies and prolonged excess stimulant use rather than from specific external threats. Paradoxically, people who are chronically frightened may seek or even create environments and situations that mirror their chemical imbalances to justify the way they feel. This creates a cyclical relationship in which chemistry provokes behavior, which produces the environment that reinforces the chemistry.

Emotional stress will exacerbate the nutritional deficiencies that induced the stress to begin with, adding momentum to the cyclical nature of the chemical imbalance. Drinking coffee or caffeine increases the stress hormone cortisol and accelerates the clearance of water-soluble vitamins, mimicking the body's chemical reaction to fear. Ironically, people increase their coffee intake to raise energy and focus to overcome "stressful" deadlines and situations. The public perception of coffee is a mirage that prevents people from recognizing that regular caffeine use causes the panicked state to begin with.

Evidence for nutrient deficiencies as the culprit for anxiety is found among elderly people. Senior citizens are more likely to possess rigid thinking and at times paralyzing fear; they are also more likely to suffer from a lack of appetite and malnourishment. People who suffer from constant fear often become too frightened to make the necessary changes to address the cause of their anxiety.

CHAPTER 5:
NUTRITION

Malnutrition is endemic to poverty. People who are malnourished show a decrease in activity levels and impaired mental function. This results in decreased productivity, reducing the chance of improving their circumstances. Studies show clear connections between lower socioeconomic status, poor housing, unemployment, broken homes, recurrent illness, and childhood malnutrition. Animal studies have shown that malnourished rats exhibit behavior and learning disabilities that persisted even after their diet was corrected. The behavioral abnormalities from malnourished reproductive rats appeared to be transmitted to succeeding generations.[48] Behavior and learning disabilities common in malnourished children can be expressed as apathy, irritability, and an inability to concentrate. The brain is specifically vulnerable to malnourishment during periods of growth, which can lead to mental illness. Even in the absence of mental illness, depressed brain activity caused by malnourishment becomes a perennial challenge to securing the skills for higher-paying jobs.[49] Malnourishment also leads to higher rates of infection, which can worsen any preexisting nutritional impairments. Recurring illness negatively affects job performance increasing the chance of bankruptcy. Nearly two-thirds of the uninsured are in families earning below 200 percent of the federal poverty guidelines (a family of five with a household income of $62,080 [2021]).[50]

Poverty, food insecurity, addiction, and depression are causes and symptoms of one another. Almost any nutritional deficiency can cause depression. Symptoms of depression include persistent sad or empty moods, a loss of interest or pleasure in everyday activities, decreased energy, fatigue, poor appetite and weight loss, increased appetite and weight gain, altered sleeping patterns, physical hyperactivity or inactivity, feelings of worthlessness, a diminished ability to think or concentrate, aches and pains, and recurrent thoughts of death or suicide.[51] The many expressions of depression listed here further support nutritional deficiencies as a leading cause of the condition.

Each vitamin and mineral is critical for every bodily function or process at some level. A vitamin or mineral deficiency presents as a syndrome. A syndrome is a disease with many symptoms. Two people may have a calcium deficiency but present different symptoms of the syndrome. Any vitamin or mineral deficiency can cause depression, and each vitamin and mineral deficiency has many symptoms; that is why weight gain and weight loss, as well as hyperactivity and inactivity, are listed as symptoms of depression.

Depression, anxiety, and fatigue can be caused by any vitamin or mineral deficiency. These three conditions are supreme obstacles to financial success and quality of life. Proper nutrition provides a person the strength and clarity to manage stress and prevent depression while having the energy and enthusiasm needed to pursue personal ambitions. This gives the individual a significant advantage for promotions, raises, and attention from senior coworkers. Ben Franklin outworked his peers by eating porridge for breakfast rather than beer, the common option at the time.[52] All areas of life are profoundly affected by an individual's health, and all areas of life affect one another. Getting and staying healthy is part of success. Therefore, paying significant attention to diet is essential for success.

The main sources for the following information are *The New Encyclopedia of Vitamins, Minerals, Supplements, and Herbs* by Nicola Reavley and *Nutrition in Perspective* by Patricia A. Kreutler.

A nutritious diet gives the body and brain what they need to function and think properly. The body requires protein, lipids, carbohydrates, fiber, water, vitamins, and minerals in the right proportions. Food directly influences gene expression. Eating whole foods will help ensure that gene activity is balanced so that the body and brain can function accurately.

Protein

Protein is derived from the Greek word *proteios*, meaning "of the first rank." Protein can be used as an energy source after carbohydrates and lipids. Proteins are made from amino acids. Proteins can be either simple or conjugated. Simple proteins are pure proteins consisting of only amino acids. Conjugated proteins are proteins combined with nonproteins.

Conjugated Proteins

Protein conjugates	Class of protein	Specific example
Protein + nucleic acids	Nucleoproteins	Chromosomes
Protein + lipids	Lipoproteins	Chylomicrons
Protein + carbohydrates	Glycoproteins	Immunoglobulins
Protein + metal Ions	Metalloproteins	Ferritin

Protein + heme group	Chromoproteins	Hemoglobin

The body uses dietary protein to make enzymes, antibodies, structural proteins (cartilage, skin, nails, hair), contractile proteins (skeletal muscle), blood proteins (hemoglobin, albumin), and various other critical macromolecules. Amino acids, the subunits of protein, are critical for every process in the body. Essential amino acids are ones the body cannot make and are required from the diet. These include isoleucine, leucine, lysine, methionine, histidine, phenylalanine, threonine, tryptophan, and valine. Cysteine and tyrosine are classified as "conditional" because they are synthesized from methionine and phenylalanine.

High protein content does not guarantee high protein quality. Eating proteins that are high in essential amino acids is more important than focusing on the number of grams of protein per serving. Foods that are considered "complete proteins" have all the essential amino acids the body needs. Most vegetable proteins are incomplete proteins. Vegetarians and vegans can have a diet of complete proteins by combining different protein sources like rice and lentils.

Complete-Protein Foods

Hemp	Buckwheat	Chia
Quinoa	Soy	Beef
Poultry	Wild game	Fish
Milk	Eggs	Pork

The body is extremely efficient at absorbing protein. Ninety percent of all protein is broken down and absorbed as amino acids. Ninety-seven percent of animal protein is broken down and absorbed, and 78 to 85 percent of protein from legumes, fruit, and vegetables is broken down and absorbed.

As socioeconomic conditions improve for a country and for individuals, protein consumption, especially from animal sources, goes up. Although protein demand is person specific, it is generally accepted that roughly a third of a gram of protein per pound is essential for optimum health.

Creatine

Creatine is mainly synthesized in the liver, pancreas, kidneys, and brain. Ninety percent of creatine is stored in the skeletal muscle. The synthesis and functionality of creatine require calcium, magnesium, manganese, methionine, glycine, and arginine. The body uses creatine to quickly recycle energy by converting ADP back to ATP.

Foods high in creatine include herring, beef, salmon, pork, ham, lamb, chicken, tuna, and cod.

Lipids

Animals deprived of fat stop growing and die. Dietary lipids are used to transport and absorb fat-soluble vitamins (A, D, E, K), insulate and protect internal tissues, and provide concentrated energy. The caloric density of fat is twice that of protein and carbohydrates. One gram of fat yields nine kilocalories of energy; carbohydrates yield four kilocalories of energy.

Fatty acids are lipids made of a hydrocarbon chain with a methyl group at one end and a carboxylic acid group at the other. Fatty acids that have no double bonds (saturated) or trans double bonds along the hydrocarbon chain are fats. Fatty acids with one or several cis double bonds along the hydrocarbon chain are unsaturated fatty acids or oils. Fats are solid at room temperature; oils are liquid. Oils or unsaturated fatty acids are different based on the number of hydrocarbons and number of cis double bonds. Most polyunsaturated fatty acids naturally occur with cis double bonds. When these oils are heated, the cis bonds are converted to trans bonds.

Trans fats tend to increase low-density lipoproteins (LDLP) and decrease high-density lipoproteins (HDL), raising the risk of cardiovascular disease. Conversely, cis fats tend to increase HDL while reducing LDLP. LDLP is considered bad cholesterol, and HDL is considered good cholesterol. Persistent excess fat consumption can in general lead to heart disease and cancer.

Classifying Fatty Acids

Number of carbon atoms	Name	Number of double bonds
4	Butyric	0
8	Caprylic	0
16	Palmitic	0
16	Palmitoleic	1
18	Stearic	0
18	Oleic	1
18	Linoleic	2
18	Linolenic	3
20	Arachidic	0
20	Arachidonic	4

Butyric, caprylic, palmitic, stearic, and arachidic are saturated fatty acids because they have no double bonds. Palmitoleic and oleic are monounsaturated fatty acids because they have one double bond. Linoleic, linolenic, and arachidonic acid are polyunsaturated fatty acids (PUFAs) because they have more than one double bond. The body can synthesize its own fatty acids, except linoleic acid, making it an essential fatty acid. Linoleic acid is necessary for normal growth and development.

THE BIOLOGY OF SUCCESS

Foods High in Linoleic Acid

Source	Amount of linoleic acid	Serving size
Safflower oil	10 grams	1 tablespoon
Sunflower seeds	9.7 grams	1 ounce
Pine nuts	9.4 grams	1 ounce
Soybean oil	8.9 grams	1 tablespoon
Sunflower oil	8.9 grams	1 tablespoon
Corn oil	7.3 grams	1 tablespoon
Pecans	6.4 grams	1 ounce
Sesame oil	5.6 grams	1 tablespoon
Brazil nuts	5.8 grams	1 ounce

Beef, lamb, chicken, milk, cheese, and eggs are also good sources of linoleic acid. The amounts vary based on how the animal was raised.

Oil	Percent of linoleic acid
Safflower	78 percent
Grape Seed	73 percent
Sunflower	68 percent
Corn	59 percent
Soybean	51 percent
Walnut	51 percent

Sesame	45 percent
Peanut	32 percent
Canola	21 percent
Olive	10 percent
Palm	10 percent
Butter	2 percent
Coconut	2 percent

The human body absorbs roughly 95 percent of dietary lipids consumed. Normal adults can absorb as much as three hundred grams a day. When the body is unable to absorb lipids, they are excreted, and the stool is often bulky, difficult to flush, pale, oily, and foul smelling. This is known as steatorrhea and is often caused by an obstruction in the gallbladder or pancreatic duct along with a decrease in pancreatic enzymes in the small intestine.

Carbohydrates

Carbohydrates are used as a quick energy source. They can also be converted to nonessential amino acids, cholesterol, nucleic acids (DNA and RNA), and lipids. Carbohydrates combine with proteins to make hormones, glycoproteins, antibodies, and immune-signaling molecules. Glycosaminoglycans (GAGs), including heparin, chondroitin, and hyaluronic acid, are long carbohydrate chains often bound with sulfur and nitrogen, which are used as a "grounding surface" for cells to attach to and grow from. GAGs are also critical for cell-to-cell signaling, preventing cells from overdividing (cancer) and facilitating nutrient absorption into the cell.

Glucose is the main energy source for the body. The liver is the principal organ for regulating glucose metabolism. Fructose and galactose that enter the liver through the portal vein are converted to glucose. Excess glucose is stored as glycogen. The liver can store 110 grams of glycogen, and the skeletal muscle can store 245 grams. Insulin lowers blood glucose by facilitating glycogen synthesis. Thyroid hormone, glucagon, and steroid hormones tend to raise blood glucose levels.

A minimum of fifty to one hundred grams of carbs are recommended per day for adults; less than fifty grams may induce harmful fat and protein catabolism. When a healthy person is fasting, their blood glucose ranges between seventy and one hundred milligrams per deciliter; and blood glucose after a meal normally rises close to 140 milligrams per deciliter. Diets high in refined carbohydrates and sugar may cause mood swings and aggravate depression. Moreover, refined carbohydrates and sugar don't have the essential nutrients for metabolism, which can lead to nutritional deficiencies. Whole grains include vitamins and minerals that are stripped in the refining process.

Whole Grains

Teff	Millet	Oats	Spelt	Barley
Sorghum	Amaranth	Quinoa	Wild rice	Corn
Wheat berries	Bulgur	Brown rice	Buckwheat	Rye

Sialic Acid

Sialic acids are a diverse family of sugar units with a nine-carbon backbone that are primarily found attached outside cells. The brain has the highest concentration of sialic acid, and it is critical for proper development.

Foods high in sialic acid include beef, beef fat, pork, lamb, ham, chicken, duck, eggs, salmon, cod, tuna, butter, milk, breast milk, and cheese.

Fiber

In the fifth century, Hippocrates recommended cooking bread with unrefined flour, and in the early nineteenth century, Sylvester Graham advocated that bran be added to the diet. The graham cracker was named after him. Otherwise, fiber has been a relatively overlooked aspect of the diet. Fiber is made of the undigested carbohydrates that pass through the GI tract. Pectin and cellulose are two common types of fiber. A diet low in fiber is associated with coronary heart disease, diabetes, colon cancer, diverticulosis, irritable bowel syndrome, and hiatus hernia. High-fiber diets can prevent diseases of the intestinal tract because fiber binds to and clears toxins along the digestive tract, including ones found in bile acids, and efficiently moves food and waste through the body. Most vegetables, complex carbohydrates, and fruit are high in fiber.

Water

Healthy adults and nearly all living organisms are made of 45–60 percent water by weight. Water regulates body temperature and is used to dissolve vitamins, hormones, carbohydrates, amino acids, carbon dioxide, urea, and electrolytes. It is critical for lubricating the eyeballs and joints. Water is essential for proper digestion, generating mucus, chewing, swallowing, and breaking down protein and carbohydrates.

Gradual water loss is a root cause of aging. Newborns are 77 percent water, and adults are 60 percent water. Water is unevenly distributed throughout the body: bone takes up 10 percent, adipose tissue 25–30 percent, and muscle 72 percent. Adults with lean muscle mass can be made of up to 72 percent water by weight, while obese adults are closer to 50 percent. Loss of only 10 percent of the water in one's body can be life threatening. Loss of 20 percent of the water in one's body is fatal.

Water input and output are equal at roughly 2.5 quarts a day. Liquids are the main source of water, followed by solid food. Cantaloupe, yogurt, oranges, apples, bananas, cucumber, tomatoes, watermelon, celery, strawberries, bell peppers, and cottage cheese are high in water.

Symptoms of Dehydration

Dry mouth	Sleepiness	Thirst	Decreased urination	Muscle weakness
Fatigue	Headaches	Dizziness	Nausea	Diarrhea
Dry skin	Rapid heart rate	Sunken eyes	Fainting	Irritability

Synergy between Vitamins and Minerals and Enzymes and Proteins

Vitamins and minerals act as coenzymes and cofactors, respectively. Many enzymes and proteins require cofactors and coenzymes to fold and function properly. Enzymes are a type of protein produced by the body. If the body is deficient in a vitamin or mineral, then the proteins and enzymes that use that vitamin or mineral will not function properly. Different proteins and enzymes require different vitamins and minerals. Moreover, it takes several enzymes and proteins to perform a necessary biological function, with many proteins or enzymes requiring a specific vitamin or mineral. This nutritional synergy is illustrated in the following examples.

1. To turn glucose into energy (ATP), the body needs thiamin, niacin, sulfur, iodine, biotin, copper, iron, pantothenic acid, phosphorus, riboflavin, and CoQ10.
2. To make glutathione, the body needs boron, magnesium, iodine, and manganese.
3. Glutathione is an antioxidant that can recycle or re-reduce vitamin C, and vitamin C can recycle or re-reduce vitamin E.
4. To make thyroid hormone, the body needs niacin, vitamin C, iodine, selenium, zinc, iron, glutathione, and vanadium, along with the hormones progesterone and cortisol.
5. For the skeletal muscle to contract, the body needs thiamin, choline, pantothenic acid, and calcium as well as the energy molecule ATP and magnesium.

These five examples highlight the need to get all the vitamins and minerals required by the body and brain to function and think properly.

Essential Vitamins and Minerals Required for Proper Health and Function

The tables below list recommended daily allowance (RDA) and suggested optimal intake (SOI).

Major Minerals

Mineral	RDA	SOI
Potassium	2,000 milligrams	2,000–5,000 milligrams
Sodium	950 milligrams	2,300 milligrams
Calcium	1,000 milligrams	1,200–1,500 mg
Magnesium	400 milligrams	500 milligrams
Phosphorus	700 milligrams	700 milligrams
Chloride*	3,400 milligrams	3,400 milligrams

*Chloride is not a mineral; it is a halide.

Trace Minerals

Mineral	RDA	SOI
Iron	12.5 milligrams	15–30 milligrams
Zinc	12 milligrams	15–30 milligrams
Copper	1.5–3.0 milligrams	3.0 milligrams
Manganese	2–5 milligrams	10 milligrams
Selenium	60 micrograms	100–200 micrograms

Vanadium	10–60 micrograms	50–100 micrograms
Chromium	50–200 micrograms	200–400 micrograms
Boron	N/A	2–7 micrograms
Molybdenum	75–250 micrograms	250 micrograms
Cobalt	1 micrograms	1 micrograms
Iodine*	150 micrograms	200 micrograms

*Iodine is not a mineral; it is a halide.

Fat-Soluble Vitamins

Vitamin	**RDA**	**SOI**
Vitamin A	1,000 micrograms	1,500 micrograms
Vitamin D	200 IUs	600 IUs
Vitamin K1	65 micrograms	300 micrograms
Vitamin K2	65 micrograms	300 micrograms
Vitamin E	65 micrograms	500 milligrams

Water-Soluble Vitamins

Vitamin	RDA	SOI
Thiamin (B1)	1.2 milligrams	5–10 milligrams
Riboflavin (B2)	1.3 milligrams	5–10 milligrams
Niacin (B3)	16 milligrams	10–100 milligrams
Pyridoxine (B6)	1.3 milligrams	2–50 milligrams
Cobalamin (B12)	2.4 micrograms	11–100 micrograms
Pantothenic acid (B5)	5 milligrams	10 milligrams
Biotin (B7)	30 micrograms	30–300 micrograms
Folic acid (B9)	400 micrograms	400 micrograms
Vitamin C	60 milligrams	100–1,000 milligrams

Calcium RDA: One Thousand Milligrams

Essential for healthy teeth and bones, muscle contractions, proper cardiac and nervous system functioning, blood pressure regulation, and blood clotting.

MICHAEL SIMMONS

Signs and Symptoms of Deficiency

Seizures	Depression	Cognitive impairment	Personality changes
Psoriasis	Dry skin	Difficulty swallowing	Fainting
Heart failure	Muscle cramps	Cataracts	Tooth decay
Numbness or tingling in extremities	Muscle weakness	Backache, stooped posture	Anxiety
Irritability	Changes in mood and behavior	Lethargy	Jitters

Foods High in Calcium
The body needs vitamin D to absorb calcium from food.

Almonds	73.9 milligrams per ounce	Spinach	240 milligrams per cup
Collard greens	220 milligrams per cup	Nonfat milk	297 milligrams per cup
Cheddar cheese	204 milligrams per ounce	Plain yogurt	415 milligrams per cup
Tofu	404 milligrams per cup	Parmesan cheese	336 milligrams per cup
Whole milk	291 milligrams per cup	Peanuts	268 milligrams per cup

Potassium RDA: Two Thousand Milligrams

Essential for water balance in the body, muscle contractions, acid-alkali balance, nerve impulse transmission, energy metabolism, carbohydrate and protein metabolism, and healthy heart and blood vessels.

Signs and Symptoms of Deficiency

Bloating	Digestion problems	Muscle cramps	Mental confusion
Inability to concentrate	Hallucinations	Unclear thinking	Heart palpitations
Tingling or numbness in arms or legs	Constipation	Extreme thirst	Frequent urination
Depression	Psychosis	Delirium	Low blood pressure
Fatigue	Muscle weakness	Difficulty breathing	Mood swings

Food High in Potassium
High sugar intake can lead to low potassium levels.

Avocado	1,067 milligrams each	Swiss chard	961 milligrams per cup
Potato	782 milligrams each	Banana	440 milligrams each
Beet greens	1,244 milligrams per cup	Seeded raisins	1,136 milligrams per cup
Peanuts	976 milligrams per cup	Orange juice	471 milligrams per cup
Coconut water	600 milligrams per cup	Ham	402 milligrams per cup

Magnesium RDA: Four Hundred Milligrams

Essential for turning food into energy, bone metabolism, glucose and fatty acid metabolism, nervous system functioning, muscle contractions, amino acid activation, and protein synthesis.

Signs and Symptoms of Deficiency

Headaches	Dizziness	Confusion	Poor concentration	Nervousness
Cardiac arrhythmias	Muscle cramping	Memory loss	Learning impairments	Anxiety
Insomnia	Depression	Hallucinations	Hyperexcitability	IQ loss
Compulsions	Cluster headaches	Migraine headaches	Delirium	Fatigue

Foods High in Magnesium

About 50 percent of dietary magnesium is absorbed. Alcohol, estrogen (birth control), diuretics (coffee is a mild diuretic), antidepressants, and heart drugs can increase one's daily magnesium requirement.

Almonds	400 milligrams per cup	Buckwheat	372 milligrams per cup
Cashew nuts	338 milligrams per cup	Peanuts	262 milligrams per cup
Wheat bran	336 milligrams per cup	Cooked spinach	148 milligrams per cup

Cooked brown rice	79.8 milligrams per cup	Pumpkin seeds	106 milligrams per cup
Yogurt	50 milligrams per cup	Black beans	120 milligrams per cup

Phosphorus RDA: Seven Hundred Milligrams

Essential for turning food into energy, mineralization of bone and teeth, absorption and transport of nutrients, glucose absorption from food, making genetic material and cell walls, and acid-base balance.

Signs and Symptoms of Deficiency

Loss of appetite	Weight gain	Bone pain	Irregular breathing
Anxiety	Fatigue	Irritability	Stiff joints
Depression	Rickets	Breathing problems	Weakness
Numbness	Tremors	Speech disorders	Mental confusion

Foods High in Phosphorus
Vitamin D increases absorption; long-term use of antacids with aluminum hydroxide may increase one's daily requirement of phosphorus.

Beef liver	1,080 milligrams per 8 ounces	Bran cereal	1,540 milligrams per 8 ounces
Oats	776 milligrams per 8 ounces	Sunflower seeds	1,476 milligrams per 8 ounces
Yogurt	326 milligrams per 8 ounces	Egg	90 milligrams each
Potato	101 milligrams each	Cheddar cheese	1,160 milligrams per 8 ounces
Peanuts	542 milligrams per 8 ounces	Wheat germ	528 milligrams per 8 ounces

Sodium RDA: Nine Hundred and Fifty Milligrams

Essential for acid-base balance, carbohydrate and protein metabolism, and the generation of nerve impulses.

Signs and Symptoms of Deficiency

Weakness	Seizures	Fatigue	Short temper
Coma	Headaches	Restlessness	Irritability
Nausea	Dizziness	Lethargy	Malaise
Low urine production	Altered personality	Apathy	Muscle cramps

Foods High in Sodium
Absorption of sodium is extremely efficient.

White bread	147 milligrams per slice	Cottage cheese	850 milligrams per 8 ounces
Ham	2,053 milligrams per 8 ounces	Chicken	115 milligrams per 8 ounces
Bagel	430 milligrams each	Feta cheese	2,498 milligrams per 8 ounces
Egg	69 milligrams each	Bran flakes	207 milligrams per 8 ounces
Green olives	926 milligrams in 10 olives	Cheddar cheese	1,408 milligrams per 8 ounces

Chloride RDA: Thirty-Four Hundred Milligrams

Essential for maintaining an acid-base balance, making stomach acid (HCl), digestion of dietary protein and B12 absorption, and activation of amylase to break down starch (complex carbohydrates).

Signs and Symptoms of Deficiency
Symptoms are similar to those of sodium deficiency.

Muscle weakness	Loss of appetite	Lethargy	Dehydration
Difficulty breathing	Nausea	Mental confusion	Slowed breathing
Paralysis	Muscle tension or spasms		

Foods High in Chloride
Absorption of chloride by the body is extremely efficient.

Celery	180 milligrams per 50 grams	Mung beans	1,260 milligrams per 100 grams
Cottage cheese	670 milligrams per 25 grams	Cheddar cheese	1,060 milligrams per 25 grams
Dried dates	290 milligrams in 6 dates	Figs	170 milligrams in 2 figs
Olives in brine	3,000 milligrams in 5 olives	Banana	80 milligrams per 100 grams
Canned foods	Amounts vary	Mayonnaise	570 milligrams per 20 grams
Processed meats	Amounts vary		

Trace Minerals

Iron RDA: Twelve and One-Half Milligrams

Essential for turning food into energy, synthesis of red blood cells (transporting oxygen through the body and carbon dioxide out of the body), cell division, protein synthesis, and safely detoxing the body of fat-soluble toxins.

Signs and Symptoms of Deficiency

Low blood pressure	Pica	Swollen tongue	Hair loss
Pale skin	Frequent infections	Heavy periods	Anxiety
Underactive thyroid	Mood disorders	ADHD	Headaches
Restless leg syndrome	Shortness of breath	Headaches	Autism
Weakness	Fatigue	Anemia	Depression

Foods High in Iron

The body uses vitamin C, vitamin A, chloride, copper, protein, and sugar to absorb iron.

Beef liver	20 milligrams per 8 ounces	Hamburger	6.9 milligrams per 8 ounces
Cooked spinach	4.0 milligrams per 8 ounces	Raisins	12 milligrams per 8 ounces
Bran flakes	10.8 milligrams per 8 ounces	Oats	7.4 milligrams per 8 ounces
Tuna	1.4 milligrams per 3 ounce can	Chicken	3.2 milligrams per 8 ounces
Cooked navy beans	5.2 milligrams per 8 ounces	Egg	1 milligram each

Zinc RDA: Twelve Milligrams

Essential for making insulin; regulating carbohydrate metabolism; red blood cell function; protein digestion; synthesis of DNA, RNA, and proteins; healing wounds; and the synthesis of collagen.

Signs and Symptoms of Deficiency

Altered sense of taste or smell	Craving salt or sugar	Diarrhea	Low energy
Chronic fatigue	Poor immunity	Infertility	Poor memory
Lack of concentration	Nerve dysfunction	ADHD	Ringing in ears

Depression	Schizophrenia	Impotence	Hair loss
Loss of appetite	Slowed thinking	Low libido	Spots on fingernails

Foods High in Zinc

The body absorbs about 30 percent of its dietary zinc intake; calcium, phytate, and dietary fiber interfere with absorption.

Pumpkin seeds	6.6 milligrams per 8 ounces	Oysters	15.6 milligrams per 6 oysters
Cooked lentils	2.4 milligrams per 8 ounces	Wheat germ	27.2 milligrams per 8 ounces
Chickpeas	2.5 milligrams per 8 ounces	Cooked lean beef	10 milligrams per 8 ounces
Cashews	7.6 milligrams per 8 ounces	Sunflower seeds	7.2 milligrams per 8 ounces
Bran flakes	5 milligrams per 8 ounces	Oats	6.2 milligrams per 8 ounces

Copper RDA: 1.5–3.0 Milligrams

Essential for iron metabolism and red blood cell formation; healthy bones, skin, and blood vessels; proper nervous and cardiovascular system function; and a healthy immune system.

Signs and Symptoms of Deficiency

Weakness	Fatigue	Frequent sickness	Memory problems
Learning problems	Difficulty walking	Sensitive to cold	Pale skin
Premature gray hair	Nerve problems	Connective tissue defects	Anemia
Heart disease	Joint pain	Muscle pain	Numbness and tingling

Foods High in Copper

Approximately 30 percent of dietary copper is absorbed; molybdenum, zinc, cadmium, and other trace minerals interfere with absorption.

Peanuts	3.18 milligrams per 8 ounces	Walnuts	1.58 milligrams per 8 ounces
Avocado	0.53 milligrams each	Wheat germ	0.88 milligrams per 8 ounces
Cooked brown rice	0.19 milligrams per 8 ounces	Almonds	1.27 milligrams per 8 ounces
Cooked lentils	0.48 milligrams per 8 ounces	Fried beef liver	3.77 milligrams per 8 ounces

Cooked spinach	0.22 milligrams per 8 ounces	Tofu	0.94 milligrams per 8 ounces

Manganese RDA: Two to Five Milligrams

Essential for energy production, the activation of superoxide dismutase, protein metabolism, bone formation, and a healthy nervous system.

Signs and Symptoms of Deficiency

Osteoporosis	Heart disease	Abnormal fat metabolism	Abnormal carbohydrate metabolism
Low fertility	Slow or impaired growth	Skeletal defects	Fat accumulation in liver
Pancreas impairment	Low immune response	Impaired digestion	Fatigue

Foods High in Manganese

Only 3–5 percent of dietary manganese is absorbed; a marginal deficiency is common.

Wheat bran	6.34 milligrams per 8 ounces	Cooked brown rice	3.36 milligrams per 8 ounces
Chickpeas	1.6 milligrams per 8 ounces	Boiled spinach	1.6 milligrams per 8 ounces
Almonds	3.06 milligrams per 8 ounces	Buckwheat	2.1 milligrams per 8 ounces
Lentils (cooked)	1.86 milligrams per 8 ounces	Whole wheat bread	0.65 milligrams per slice
Green peas	0.8 milligrams per 8 ounces	Raisins	0.48 milligrams per 8 ounces

Selenium RDA: Sixty Micrograms

Essential for glutathione function, a healthy immune and cardiovascular system, and hormone production.

Signs and Symptoms of Deficiency

Cancer	Heart disease	Arthritis	Cataracts
Autoimmune disease	Birth defects	Fatigue	Weakness
Mental fog	Hair loss	Infertility	Goiter
Miscarriage	Hypothyroidism	Depression	Anxiety

| Cognitive decline | Psychosis | Impaired spatial learning and memory | Myopathy |

Foods High in Selenium

Organic selenium is absorbed better than inorganic selenium. Vitamin E and selenium are more effective together.

Brazil nuts	840 micrograms per 6–8 nuts	Animal kidneys	185–271 micrograms per 8 ounces
Tuna	92 micrograms per 3 ounce can	Turkey (dark meat)	54.3 micrograms per 8 ounces
Wheat germ	87.6 micrograms per 8 ounces	Rolled oats	26.2 micrograms per 8 ounces
Pork chops	117 micrograms per 8 ounces	Oysters	60.1 micrograms per 6 oysters
Egg	15 micrograms each	Cottage cheese	22 micrograms per 8 ounces
Chicken	56 micrograms per 8 ounces	Cooked mushrooms	19 micrograms per 8 ounces

Vanadium RDA: Ten to Sixty Micrograms

Essential for blood sugar, lipid and cholesterol metabolism, bone and tooth development, fertility, thyroid function, hormone production, and neurotransmitter metabolism.

Signs and Symptoms of Deficiency

Infertility	Low red blood cell production	Iron metabolism defects	Impaired bone and tooth growth
Lower milk production	Improper cartilage formation	High cholesterol	High triglycerides
Susceptibility to cancer	Susceptibility to heart disease	Diabetes	Increased blood lipids
Increased size of thyroid	Impaired hormone production	Impaired neurotransmitter metabolism	Increased spontaneous abortion rates

Only 5–10 percent of vanadium is absorbed from food; it is stored primarily in fat and bone.

Foods high in vanadium include mushrooms, shellfish, black pepper, parsley, dill weed, root vegetables, vegetable oils, nuts, lettuce, strawberries, whole grains, and cereals

Chromium RDA: Fifty to Two Hundred Micrograms

Essential for normal sugar and fat metabolism; it is believed to be a cofactor for insulin.

Signs and Symptoms of Deficiency

High blood fat	High blood cholesterol	Diabetes	Heart disease

THE BIOLOGY OF SUCCESS

Weight loss	Neuropathy	Fatigue	Muscle weakness
Growth delays	Low HDL	High blood pressure	High triglycerides
Worsened depression	Worsened schizophrenia	Anxiety	Sugar cravings

Foods High in Chromium

Chromium is poorly absorbed through food. Antacids may decrease absorption.

Brown sugar	34 micrograms per 100 grams	Ham	26 micrograms per 100 grams
Wheat bran	19 micrograms per 100 grams	Cheddar cheese	24 micrograms per 100 grams
Split peas	13 micrograms per 100 grams	Wheat germ	13 micrograms per 100 grams
Brown lentils	13 micrograms per 100 grams	Broccoli	22 micrograms per 8 ounces
Grapes/ grape juice	8 micrograms per 8 ounces	Garlic	3 micrograms per teaspoon

Boron RDA: No established RDA

Essential for healthy bones and joints.

Signs and Symptom of Deficiency

Abnormal limb development	Osteoporosis	Kidney stones	Decreased awareness
Osteoarthritis	Inflammation	Increased risk of prostate, lung, and cervical cancer	Poor memory
Muscle weakness	Stomach and digestive parasites	Candida infection	Eye infections
Hormone imbalance	Diabetes	Skin infections	Impaired cognitive development

Foods High in Boron
Boron is absorbed well through food.

Prune juice	1.43 micrograms per 8 ounces	Avocado	1.07 milligrams per 4 ounces
Raisins	0.95 milligrams per 1.5 ounces	Peaches	0.80 milligrams each
Grape juice	0.76 milligrams per 8 ounces	Apple	0.66 milligrams each
Peanuts	0.48 milligrams per ounce	Chickpeas	0.92 milligrams per 130 grams

| Almonds | 0.42 milligrams per 15 grams | Pear | 0.48 milligrams each |

Molybdenum RDA: 75–250 Micrograms

Essential for removing the waste products of protein metabolism, iron utilization, and carbohydrate metabolism alcohol and sulfite detoxification.

Signs and Symptoms of Deficiency

Rapid heart rate	Rapid breathing	Headache	Night blindness
Anemia	Mental disturbances	Nausea	Vomiting
Coma	Seizures	Opisthotonos (muscle spasms causing backward arching of the head, neck, and spine)	Lens dislocation

Foods High in Molybdenum

Eighty-eight to ninety-three percent of molybdenum is absorbed. Copper reduces molybdenum absorption.

Black-eyed peas	288 micrograms per half cup	Beef liver	104 micrograms per 3 ounces
Lima beans	104 micrograms per half cup	Plain yogurt	26 micrograms per cup
2 percent milk	22 micrograms per cup	Baked potato	16 micrograms in one medium baked potato
Oats	180 micrograms per 100 grams	Raisin bran	76 micrograms per 100 grams
Bread	21mcg per 100 grams	Banana	8 micrograms per 100 grams

Cobalt RDA: One Microgram

It is a cofactor for vitamin B12, the synthesis of DNA, the production of red blood cells, the maintenance of nerve function, and the detoxification of cyanide.

Signs and symptoms of deficiency, as well as foods high in cobalt, are the same as those for vitamin B12. Dietary cobalt can be utilized only as cobalamin, or vitamin B12. Inorganic cobalt is excreted and has no known function.

THE BIOLOGY OF SUCCESS

Iodine RDA: 150 Micrograms

Iodine is needed for normal metabolism, growth and development, and proper thyroid function; it is a cofactor for thyroid hormones.

Signs and Symptoms of Deficiency

Cretinism	Goiter	Hypothyroidism	Fatigue
Apathy	Drowsiness	Sensitivity to cold	Muscle weakness
Weight gain	Flaky skin	Miscarriage	Fibrocystic breast disease
Mental delays	Learning disabilities	Poor motivation	Breast cancer

Foods High in Iodine

The body absorbs iodine with nearly 100 percent efficiency.

Mackerel	255 micrograms per 150 grams	Mussels	180 micrograms per 150 grams
Cod	165 micrograms per 150 grams	Yogurt	95 micrograms per 150 grams
Milk	86 micrograms per 560 grams	Eggs	37 micrograms each
Liver	22 micrograms per 150 grams	Bacon	13 micrograms per 265 grams

Fat-Soluble Vitamins

Vitamin A RDA: 1,000–1,500 Micrograms

Essential for vision, especially in low light, and healthy teeth, bones, skin, reproductive system, and epithelial cells. Vitamin A is known as the antimicrobial vitamin because of its efficacy against infection. It is essential for cellular growth, repair, and differentiation.

Signs and Symptoms of Deficiency

Dry skin	Night blindness	Retarded growth	Cancer
Increased infection	Acne	Poor wound healing	Infertility
Dry eyes	Thick, scaly skin	Slowed learning	Sleep disturbances
Weight gain	Diabetes	Lethargy	Thyroid disorders
Dandruff	Ear infections	Flaky skin	Cystic acne

Foods High in Vitamin A
Dietary fat is necessary for absorption.

Winter or butternut squash	22,869 IUs per 8 ounces	Sweet potato	21,907 IUs each
Kale	10,302 IUs per 8 ounces	Carrots	10,190 IUs each
Beef liver	71,048 IUs per 8 ounces	Spinach	2,813 IUs per 8 ounces
Boiled pumpkin	264 IUs per 8 ounces	Egg	84 IUs each

| Mangoes | 805 IUs each | Broccoli | 226 IUs per 8 ounces |

Vitamin D RDA: Two Hundred IUs

Essential for the regulation and absorption of calcium and phosphorus, proper bone and tooth development, normal cell growth and maturation, a healthy nervous and immune system, and regulating hormones. Deficiency is common.

Signs and Symptoms of Deficiency

Insomnia	Osteoporosis	Heart disease	Cancer
Autoimmune disease	Depression	Diabetes	Arthritis
Autism	Schizophrenia	Fatigue	Bone and back pain
Impaired wound healing	Cognitive impairment	Dementia	Neurotransmitter imbalance
Psoriasis	Chronic pain	Seasonal affective disorder	Rickets

Foods High in Vitamin D

Absorption requires dietary fat. Cholesterol in the skin is converted to vitamin D when exposed to the U.V. rays in sunlight.

Tuna	269 IUs per 3.5 ounce can	Oysters	269 IUs per 6 oysters
Shiitake mushrooms	249 IUs per 4 mushrooms	Natural raisin bran	45.6 IUs per 30 grams
Fresh salmon	352–1,257 IUs per 8 ounces	Canned herring	754 IUs per 8 ounces
Eggs	25 IUs each	Shrimp	342 IUs per 8 ounces
Sardines	2,628–3,588 IUs per 8 ounces	Cod liver oil	1,275 IUs per tablespoon

Vitamin K$_1$ (Phylloquinone) RDA: Sixty-Five Micrograms

Essential for blood clotting, bone metabolism, heart and kidney function, and wound healing. Deficiency is rare.

Signs and Symptoms of Deficiency

Easy bruising	Easy bleeding	Osteoporosis	Heavy menstrual periods
Blood in stool	Blood in urine	Nosebleeds	Depression
Diabetes	Wrinkles	Weakness	Increased fractures

Cardiovascular disease	Alzheimer's disease	Cognitive decline	Lower IQ

Foods High in Vitamin K_1
Absorption requires dietary fat and bile in the gut.

Kale	1.062 micrograms per 8 ounces	Spinach	890 micrograms per 8 ounces
Turnip greens	530 micrograms per 8 ounces	Broccoli	400 micrograms per 8 ounces
Avocado	160 micrograms per 8 ounces	Cabbage	96 micrograms per 8 ounces
Beef liver	208 micrograms per 8 ounces	Green tea	19 micrograms per teaspoon

Vitamin K_2 RDA: Sixty-Five Micrograms

Essential for preventing calcium from building up in soft tissues (especially arteries), heart function, and proper bone development.

Signs and Symptoms of Deficiency

Easy bruising	Heavy menstrual periods	Blood in urine	Bleeding from GI tract
Oozing from nose or gums	Cancer	Hormone imbalance	Kidney stones
Obesity	Diabetes	Rheumatoid arthritis	Tooth decay
Vascular disease	Bone loss	Plaque formation	Nausea when eating fatty foods
Calcium buildup in soft tissue	Insomnia	Anxiety	Depression

Foods High in Vitamin K_2
Absorption requires dietary fat and bile in the gut.

Natto	313 micrograms per ounce	Beef liver	72 micrograms per slice
Chicken (dark meat)	51 micrograms per 3 ounces	Hard cheese	25 micrograms per ounce
Ground beef	8 micrograms per 3 ounces	Whole milk	3.2 micrograms per 8 ounces

Canadian bacon	3 micrograms per 3 ounces	Chicken liver	3.6 micrograms per ounce

Vitamin K2 (menaquinone) is a group of vitamins found in bacteria and in animals; it is a by-product of bacteria metabolism. Bacterial flora in the intestine synthesize 50–60 percent of the vitamin K2 in the body, and the remainder is from food sources.[53]

Vitamin E RDA: Fifteen Milligrams

Essential for removing free radicals; protecting fats, cell membranes, and DNA from oxidative stress; and heart function.

Signs and Symptoms of Deficiency

Loss of balance	Lethargy	Anemia	Cancer
Heart disease	Premature aging	Vision problems	Loss of feeling in arms and legs
Muscle pain and weakness	Fertility issues	Hormone imbalances	Weight gain
Depression	Dry skin	Wrinkles	Anxiety

Foods High in Vitamin E
Absorption requires dietary fat and bile in the gut.

Wheat germ	47 milligrams per 8 ounces	Sunflower seeds	46.6 milligrams per 8 ounces
Peanuts	12.6 milligrams per 8 ounces	Almonds	58.4 milligrams per 8 ounces
Cooked spinach	3.7 milligrams per 8 ounces	Avocado	3.1 milligrams per 8 ounces
Hazelnuts	33.6 milligrams per 8 ounces	Turnip greens	2.7 milligrams per 8 ounces
Butternut squash	2.7 milligrams per 8 ounces	Trout	16 milligrams per 3 ounces

Water-Soluble Vitamins

Thiamin (Vitamin B1) RDA: 1.2 Milligrams

Essential for the metabolism of fat and carbohydrates; healthy growth; healthy hair, skin, and muscles; a healthy brain and nervous system; and alcohol metabolism.

Signs and Symptoms of Deficiency

Burning feet	Rapid weight loss	Poor appetite	Colitis
Nerve damage	Nerve inflammation	Fatigue	Loss of short-term memory
Confusion	Depression	Apathy	Irritability

Cardiovascular problems	Korsakoff syndrome	High pain tolerance	Muscle cramps
Enlarged heart	Paralysis	Reduced mental function	Strange eye movements

Foods High in Thiamin

Daily intake is necessary; alcohol reduces thiamin absorption.

Pork	1.23 milligrams per pork chop	Oats	1.19 milligrams per 8 ounces
Cooked white beans	0.53 milligrams per 8 ounces	Cooked black beans	0.58 milligrams per 8 ounces
Sunflower seeds	2 milligrams per 8 ounces	Cooked lentils	0.53 milligrams per 8 ounces
Cod	0.16 milligrams per fillet	Brazil nuts	0.28 milligrams per 6–8 nuts
Wheat germ	1.08 milligrams per 8 ounces	Dried mung beans	1.26 milligrams per 8 ounces

Riboflavin (Vitamin B2) RDA: 1.3 Milligrams

Essential for turning food into energy; normal growth and development; a healthy immune system; healthy skin, hair, and blood cells; hormone function; and a healthy nervous system and brain.

Signs and Symptoms of Deficiency

Itchy eyes	Light sensitivity	Cracking around the mouth	Burning lips, mouth, and tongue
Flaky, peeling skin, especially around the nose, eyebrows, chin, and cheeks	Behavioral changes	Nervousness	Depression
Swelling or soreness around the throat	Swollen magenta tongue	Digestive problems	Dermatitis
Fatigue	Anemia	Cataracts	Greasy, scaly skin

Foods High in Riboflavin

Daily intake is necessary; alcohol, antidepressants, and estrogen (birth control) may increase one's daily riboflavin requirement.

Almonds	1.96 milligrams per 8 ounces	Lamb liver	4.03 milligrams per 100 grams

Scallops	0.85 milligrams per 6 ounces	Canned pink salmon	0.175 milligrams 3.25 ounce can
Cooked spinach	0.42 milligrams per 8 ounces	Wheat germ	0.58 milligrams per 8 ounces
Natural yogurt	0.6 milligrams per 8 ounces	Milk	0.4 milligrams per 8 ounces
Egg	0.2 milligrams each	Cooked quinoa	0.2 milligrams per 8 ounces

Niacin (Vitamin B3) RDA: Sixteen Milligrams

Essential for turning food into energy; healthy skin, blood cells, and digestive system; normal growth and development; hormone production; healthy brain and nervous system; repairing genetic material; and protecting genes from viruses.

Signs and Symptoms of Deficiency

Tremors	Hallucinations	Death	Poor concentration
Headache	Diarrhea	Dermatitis	Depression
Apathy	Delusions	Memory loss	Sore mouth
Weakness	Disorientation	Anxiety	Fatigue
Digestion disorders	Scaly rash when exposed to sunlight	Swollen mouth	Bright red tongue

Foods High in Niacin

Daily intake is necessary; the body can turn the amino acid tryptophan into niacin.

Canned tuna	21.9 milligrams per 5.8 ounce can	Canned salmon	59.4 milligrams per 8 ounces
All bran	33.4 milligrams per 8 ounces	Peanuts	16.7 milligrams per 8 ounces
Chicken	19.2 milligrams per 8 ounces	Lamb liver	12.2 milligrams per 100 grams
Wheat germ	7.8 milligrams per 8 ounces	Cooked brown rice	3 milligrams per 8 ounces
Avocado	2.6 milligrams per 8 ounces	Sunflower seeds	3.8 milligrams per 8 ounces

Pantothenic Acid (Vitamin B5) RDA: Five Milligrams

Essential for turning food into energy, cholesterol and fatty acid metabolism, healthy red blood cells, a healthy immune system, healthy adrenal function, and healthy nervous system.

Signs and Symptoms of Deficiency

Depression	Fatigue	Irritability	Insomnia
Stomach pains	Vomiting	Burning feet	Upper respiratory infections

High blood cholesterol	Rheumatoid arthritis	Hypoglycemia	Graying and loss of hair
Constipation	Exhaustion	Duodenal ulcers	Dizziness
Low blood pressure	Muscle weakness	Increased infection	Low antibody production

Foods High in Pantothenic Acid

Daily intake is recommended. It can be stored in the liver. Sulfa drugs (antibiotics), sleeping pills, estrogen (birth control), and alcohol may raise one's daily pantothenic acid requirement.

Egg	1.1 milligrams each	Avocado	2.2 milligrams each
Cooked collard greens	0.950 milligrams per 8 ounces	Banana	0.45 milligrams each
Cooked beef liver	5.03 milligrams per 85 grams	Roast chicken	2.94 milligrams per 8 ounces
Raw mushrooms	1.46 milligrams per 8 ounces	Wheat germ	2.84 milligrams per 8 ounces
Cooked lentils	1.2 milligrams per 8 ounces	Peanuts	2.46 milligrams per 8 ounces

Biotin (Vitamin B7) RDA: Thirty Micrograms

Essential for turning food into energy, protein metabolism, making genetic material, healthy hair, and a healthy immune system.

Signs and Symptoms of Deficiency

Fatigue	Alopecia	Scaly rash around eyes and nose	Depression
Lethargy	Hallucinations	Numbness and tingling in extremities	Ataxia
Unusual facial fat distribution	Muscle pain	Nausea	Loss of appetite
Paresthesia	Insomnia	High cholesterol	Impaired immune system
Grayish, dry skin	Conjunctivitis	Brittle nails	Seborrheic dermatitis

Foods High in Biotin

Daily intake is recommended. Biotin can also be absorbed from intestinal bacteria (probiotics). Sulfa drugs (antibiotics), estrogen (birth control), and alcohol may increase one's daily biotin requirement.

Beef liver	82 micrograms per 3 ounces	Cooked oatmeal	58 micrograms per 8 ounces
Baked salmon	10 micrograms per 3 ounces	Cooked brown rice	18 micrograms per 8 ounces
Roasted peanuts	39 micrograms per 100 grams	Chocolate	32 micrograms per 100 grams

Dried peas	18 micrograms per 100 grams	Mushrooms	16 micrograms per 100 grams
Cauliflower	17 micrograms per 100 grams	Molasses	9 micrograms per 100 grams

Pyridoxine (Vitamin B6) RDA: 1.3 Milligrams

Essential for turning food into energy; a healthy cardiovascular, nervous, and immune system; protein metabolism and hormone production; healthy skin, hair, and blood cells; making genetic material; and converting tryptophan into niacin.

Signs and Symptoms of Deficiency

Changes in mood	Irritability	Anxiety	Depression
Muscle pain	Low energy	Cracked or sore lips	Peripheral neuropathy
Seizures	Inflammation of the tongue	Ulcers of the mouth	Pellagra-like syndrome
Microcytic anemia	Muscle weakness	Difficulty walking	Nausea
Neuritis	Severe convulsions	Cancer	Diabetes

Foods High in Pyridoxine and Vitamin B6
Daily intake is necessary.

Beef liver	0.569 milligrams per 3 ounces	Banana	0.480 milligrams each
Avocado	0.840 micrograms each	Chicken	0.340 micrograms per 3 ounces
White potato	200 micrograms each	Wheat germ	1.42 milligrams per 8 ounces
Canned tuna	0.9 milligrams per 3 ounces	Cooked spinach	0.42 milligrams per 8 ounces
Raisins	0.34 milligrams per 8 ounces	Wheat bran	0.72 milligrams per 8 ounces

Folacin, Folic Acid, or Vitamin B9 RDA: Four Hundred Micrograms

Essential for making genetic material; protein metabolism; healthy red blood cells, bones, and hair; and a healthy nervous, digestive, and immune system.

Signs and Symptoms of Deficiency

Megaloblastic anemia	GI disturbances	Tongue lesions	Changes in mood
Irritability	Premature graying of hair	Development problems	Bloating

Chronic fatigue syndrome	Depression	Gingivitis	Schizophrenia
Glossitis (inflammation of the tongue)	Dementia	Loss of appetite	Poor immune system
Shortness of breath	Heart disease	Colorectal cancer	Anxiety

Foods High in Folic Acid

Daily intake is recommended. Some folic acid can be stored in the liver. Tobacco, alcohol, estrogen (birth control), and antiseizure medications may increase one's daily folic acid requirement.

Brewer's yeast	0.313 milligrams per tablespoon	Cooked beef liver	0.123 milligrams per 3 ounces
Raw spinach	0.106 milligrams per 8 ounces	Cooked beets	0.132 milligrams per 8 ounces
Cooked lentils	0.340 milligrams per 8 ounces	Cooked black-eyed peas	0.340 milligrams per 8 ounces
Avocado	0.124 milligrams each	Cooked asparagus	0.876 milligrams per 4 spears
Almonds	0.792 milligrams per 8 ounces	Orange juice	0.713 milligrams per 8 ounces

Cobalamin (Vitamin B12) RDA: 2.4 Micrograms

Essential for turning food into energy; protein and fat metabolism; healthy nerves, blood cells, skin, and hair; production of genetic material; and proper growth and development.

Signs and Symptoms of Deficiency

Obsessive-compulsive disorder	Impotence	Psychosis	Memory loss
Delusions	Anxiety	Paranoia	Personality changes
Apathy	Sleep disturbances	Confusion	Violent behavior
Tinnitus	Ataxia	Tremors	Disturbances in taste and smell
Impaired pain perception	Paresthesia	Depression	Bladder or bowel incontinence

Foods High in Cobalamin and Vitamin B12
Daily intake is recommended. Absorption requires intrinsic factor (a glycoprotein in the stomach); antacids, alcohol, estrogen (birth control), and sleeping pills may increase one's daily cobalamin requirement.

Beef liver	68 micrograms per 3 ounces	Clams	99 micrograms per 3.5 ounce can
Sauerkraut	32 micrograms per can	Peach	7 micrograms each

Trout	4.64 micrograms per fillet	Tuna	4.38 micrograms per 8 ounces
Beef steak	2.11 micrograms per 100 grams	Haddock	2.08 micrograms per fillet
Cottage cheese	1.36 micrograms per 8 ounces	Pink salmon	4.29 micrograms per half fillet

Vitamin C RDA: Sixty Milligrams

Essential for making collagen (a protein), the connective tissue required by bones, cartilage, and teeth; healing wounds; a healthy immune and nervous system; adrenal hormone production, and eye health. It also acts as an antioxidant to prevent disease.

Signs and Symptoms of Deficiency

Easy bruising	Swollen gums	Digestive disorders	Swollen, painful joints
Dry, scaly skin	Depression	High blood pressure	Impaired spatial memory
Sugar cravings	Anxiety	Impaired immune system	Nosebleeds
Slow wound healing	Fluid retention	Diabetes	Cataracts
Cancer	Cardiovascular disease	Swollen limbs	Weakness

Foods High in Vitamin C

Daily intake is required; smoking, pollutants, aspirin, alcohol, estrogen, antibiotics, and steroids may increase one's daily vitamin C requirement.

Raw red peppers	174 milligrams per 8 ounces	Orange juice	124 milligrams per 8 ounces
Black currants	202 milligrams per 8 ounces	Grapefruit juice	94 milligrams per 8 ounces
Boiled kohlrabi	89 milligrams per 8 ounces	Lemons	83 milligrams each
Strawberries	82 milligrams per 8 ounces	Green peppers	82 milligrams per 8 ounces
Guavas	165 milligrams each	Papaya	86 milligrams per 8-ounce cube

CoQ10

CoQ10 is not considered an essential nutrient because it is synthesized in the liver using the same pathway as cholesterol. It is sometimes recommended that people who take a statin supplement with CoQ10. Coenzyme Q is found in all plant and animal cells. The body can convert dietary CoQ6 and CoQ8 into CoQ10. Levels of CoQ10 decline with age. A CoQ10 deficiency can contribute to or cause cancer, muscular dystrophy, diabetes, obesity, periodontal disease, lowered immune function, and neurodegenerative disorders, including Parkinson's disease. CoQ10 is used in the mitochondria to make ATP, the body's main energy molecule, and is particularly important for proper heart function. Meat, fish, vegetable oils, broccoli, and spinach are primary sources of CoQ10.

Impacts of Diet on Behavior
Malnutrition and specific vitamin or mineral deficiencies can dramatically influence perception, personality, and behavior. Behavioral disorders from nutritional deficiencies can be expressed as personality quirks or severe obstacles to normal social integration. People commonly overlook character as a result of dietary permutations. This leads to subjective and at times hostile opinions toward others and oneself. Subjective analysis is a symptom of ignorance. A person's behavior, temperament, intelligence, and optimism are dramatically influenced by diet. Diet is the link between nurture and nature.

CHAPTER 6:
BEHAVIORAL DISORDERS

The most significant determinant of success or failure is behavior. An individual's daily habits and core beliefs will decide the outcome of their life. For most people, habits and beliefs change with time, experience, and education. However, there are individuals who suffer from behavioral disorders that significantly interfere with the natural processes of growth and development. Behavioral disorders are likely developed in utero or during childhood and in most cases are the product of severe nutritional deficiencies and imbalances. Behavioral disorders limit or prevent both physical and mental growth and development. This observation supports the unity of matter and consciousness. Where there is an error in thinking, there is an imbalance in chemistry. Variations in behavioral disorders result from variations in nutritional imbalances. In his book *Nutrient Power*, William Walsh establishes clear connections between the expression of different behavioral disorders and specific nutrient abnormalities.

Intermittent explosive disorder (IED) manifests in people who are well behaved and cooperative but have occasional explosions of uncontrolled rage that can last for fifteen to twenty minutes. These outbursts can result in assault and property damage and often end with a sense of remorse and pleas for forgiveness. Ninety percent of people with IED have very elevated levels of copper and zinc.

Oppositional defiant disorder (ODD) is diagnosed in people who are opposed to authority and are overly stubborn, argumentative, and controlling. They have a hard time making friends and are known for physically assaulting people. People with ODD are often undermethylated and have low dopamine and serotonin levels. As children, they are commonly prescribed Ritalin or other ADHD medications.

Conduct disorder (CD) is diagnosed in individuals who aggressively act out toward people and animals. They participate in behaviors like stealing, lying, bullying, and fighting. These individuals are more likely to abuse drugs and alcohol and engage in sexual activity at an early age. Severe pyrrole disorder and undermethylation are signatures of this type of behavioral disorder. (See the sections below on pyrrole and methylation.)

Antisocial personality disorder (ASPD) is characterized by extreme narcissism, hypersexuality, and a high pain threshold. Those diagnosed with ASPD may have good verbal skills and often have engaging personalities. People with ASPD disregard laws and social norms, engage in impulsive actions without regard for consequences, have low opinions of "normal" people, and commonly believe them to be cowards. This type of personality is created by undermethylation, pyrrole disorder, elevated toxic metals, severe zinc deficiencies, and low to normal copper levels.

Attention-deficit/hyperactivity disorder (ADHD) is an umbrella term for several behavioral or learning disorders, including predominantly inattentive, predominantly impulsive and hyperactive, and a combination of hyperactive/impulsive and inattentive disorders.

Predominantly inattentive individuals often have normal to high intelligence and poor focus and concentration. They are often described as "space cadets" with excellent behavioral control and social skills. People with this type of ADHD commonly suffer from deficiencies in folic acid, B12, zinc, and choline.

Predominantly impulsive and hyperactive disorder is diagnosed in people who tend to be in constant motion and highly distractible, with short attention spans. People with this disorder academically underperform regardless of their intelligence. Metal metabolism disorder, copper overload, and a zinc deficiency are common among those with this type of behavioral disorder.

Combined hyperactive/impulsive and inattentive disorder is the largest subtype of ADHD. Individuals in this group often suffer from more severe academic underachievement than those in the other two groups. Several chemical imbalances are indicated by this disorder, including copper and zinc imbalances, methylation abnormalities, and pyrrole disorders.

Pyrroles

Pyrroles are cyclical structures in bile pigments, B12, and heme groups that are found in hemoglobin and cytochromes. They are a by-product of hemoglobin and considered toxic in high levels. An excess number of pyrroles may indicate liver dysfunction.

Methylation

The methylation patterns of DNA determine gene expression. If a gene (DNA that codes for a specific protein) is overmethylated, it is less likely to be expressed (transcribed into mRNA and translated into a protein). Conversely, if it is undermethylated, it is more likely to be expressed. Over- and undermethylated genes can negatively affect a person and influence their personality. Someone whose genes are inappropriately undermethylated is more likely to develop cancer. In terms of personality, people who are undermethylated are often perfectionists, strong willed, and highly accomplished. They can also express symptoms of OCD and suffer from seasonal allergies. People who are overmethylated tend to have excellent social skills and many friendships and are noncompetitive and artistic. Overmethylated individuals also tend to have food sensitivities and suffer from anxiety. DNA methylation patterns are influenced by diet. Folic acid, SAMe, methionine, taurine, vitamin C, vitamin E, glutathione, cysteine, and niacin (B3) increase methyl groups.[54]

Behavioral disorders and personality are substantially influenced and created by diet. The examples illustrated above are extreme cases of atypical behaviors. However, they help reveal the impact diet has on temperament, personality, and even perception. The abilities to work with others, follow instructions, and focus are bedrock skills required for success. These attributes are refined or impaired through diet. Each person has their own strengths and weaknesses that ebb and flow based in part on the food they eat. Moreover, people can slowly develop behavioral disorders by persistently overlooking critical nutrients.

CHAPTER 7:
BEHAVIOR AND ADDICTION

> Drug: Any substance, natural or synthetic, that has a physiological effect on a living body when used for the treatment of disease, the alleviation of pain, recreation, or self-indulgence, leading in some cases to progressive addiction.
>
> –CHAMBERS DICTIONARY OF SCIENCE AND TECHNOLOGY.[55]

Drug addiction will slowly change a person's behavior. A drug user's awareness gradually contracts until all they can think about is getting high. This creates a type of tunnel vision that is often supported by their ability to rationalize poor decisions. They ignore responsibilities like paying rent or showing up for work by reclassifying these activities as nonessential or simply as obstacles to getting high. The visible changes in behavior are manifestations of the drug's ability to alter the user's perception. Users become addicts slowly, and the shift in perception goes undetected in only small irregularities in behavior, with the cumulative effect often ending in poverty. This scenario usually occurs with illegal drug and alcohol addiction. However, any substance that interferes with the body's natural biochemistry and has a cumulative addictive effect can negatively affect a person's health and the quality of their life.

The most common addictions are to caffeine, nicotine, cannabis, and alcohol. Caffeine interferes with collagen synthesis and prevents the user from feeling tired by binding to ADP receptors, which can cause insomnia. Caffeine also raises cortisol levels, accelerates skin aging, increases symptoms of depression, and interferes with vitamin and mineral absorption. Cigarettes increase the chance of cardiovascular disease, cancer, inflammatory bowel syndrome, periodontal disease, and liver disorders and cause vitamin and mineral deficiencies, especially deficiencies of antioxidants like vitamin C and vitamin E. Cannabis is a psychoactive drug that can impair memory and executive functions and increase the chance of psychosis. Persistent alcohol use produces a disease state in every organ it comes in contact with.

It is estimated that 7 percent of adults living in the United States have a drinking problem. The damage drinking does to the body is substantial. It affects every system in the body, especially the digestive, nervous, circulatory, endocrine, and muscular systems. Cancers of the mouth, tongue, esophagus, and pharynx can be alcohol related. Alcohol abuse can cause inflammation of the pancreas and small intestine. Liver dysfunction, specifically cirrhosis, is a common disease among alcoholics. Cirrhosis happens when healthy cells are replaced by scar tissue, a condition thought to be permanent.[56]

Alcohol interferes with vitamin and mineral metabolism. It inhibits vitamin A absorption; causes a deficiency in B vitamins, zinc, and magnesium; lowers the level of antioxidants like selenium and vitamin C; and interferes in the activation of vitamin D, which can cause a deficiency in calcium and phosphate. Excess alcohol consumption can lead to a severe thiamin and niacin deficiency, resulting in Korsakoff syndrome.[57] This is a condition with many symptoms, including psychosis and skeletal muscle dysfunction expressed as a stupor and tremors. Some experts recommend supplements of one hundred milligrams of thiamin to anyone who consumes alcohol in excess.

Drinking alcohol doesn't make someone an alcoholic. In their book *Brain Allergies*, William Philpott and Dwight K. Kalita propose that addiction is a type of allergy.[58] Allergies affect people differently, which may help explain why some people are prone to drug addiction. People can have allergic addictions to foods, chemicals, narcotics, tobacco, coffee, and alcohol. Seventy-five percent of people are allergic to tobacco after their first use. The initial allergic symptoms of tobacco can include nausea, dizziness, and a cough. What makes these allergens addictive is the withdrawal phase of the drug. Philpott and Kalita claim that the phase of withdrawal from the addicted substance is a sign of allergy symptoms reemerging. As soon as the substance is consumed, the allergy symptoms stop. The allergy symptoms are part of the body's detox process. A healthy, well-balanced body may experience adaptive addiction, in which the body can repair itself quickly, preventing an allergic addiction dependency. However, if these people incur any additional physical or emotional stress, seasonal allergies, or severe infection, their bodies' tolerance or recovery potential will fail, leading to a state of addiction. This creates the paradox of people craving what they are allergic to. As long as there is allergen residue in the liver, the body will have a subtle impulse to continue the addiction.

For most people, life is hard enough without being addicted to drugs or alcohol. The burden of addiction weighs heavily on a person's career and earning power, as it damages the brain and impairs perception. A person is unable to express their full potential and often suffers depression and remorse, which can lead the way toward poverty. Homelessness is the nadir of addiction. The National Coalition for the

Homeless has found that 38 percent of homeless people are alcohol dependent, and 26 percent are dependent on other harmful chemicals.[59] Drug and alcohol addicts are not forthcoming about their addictions, so these percentages are likely higher.

Alcohol and drug use is not confined to low-income households. Dual purchasers of alcohol and tobacco in the United Kingdom appear to be distributed evenly among income groups.[60] However, tobacco and alcohol expenditure appears to exacerbate poverty in low-income households in the United Kingdom. Hundreds of thousands of additional households in the United Kingdom would be defined as living in relative poverty on their income after subtracting their tobacco and alcohol expenditure.[61] The contrast between economic classes is the financial burden and dependency of consumption. By appearance tobacco and alcohol use are ancillary to the economically stable while creating obsequious low-income users. The ability for one person to use alcohol and legal drugs for enjoyment while another uses them to cope with everyday stress may be diet related.

Wealthy households tend to place a higher value on healthy, nutrient-dense foods while poorer households tend to value unhealthy ones. Higher-income households (making more than $70,000 a year) are willing to pay almost double for the daily recommended quantity of vegetables and nearly three times more for the daily recommended quantity of fruit. By contrast, low-income households (making less than $25,000 a year) are willing to pay more for sugar and saturated fat.[62] Eating healthily helps mitigate the damage done by drugs and alcohol while preventing the people who have an adaptive addiction from developing an addiction dependency.

CHAPTER 8:
EATING BEHAVIOR

Eating habits determine the function of the body and brain. Every essential nutrient is critical for every function of the body and brain. There are clear contrasts in diet between economic classes. Low-income people are reportedly less likely to consume a healthy diet than wealthier people, and energy-dense (high-calorie), nutrient-poor diets are preferentially consumed by persons of lower socioeconomic status.[63]

The first assumption of this dichotomy in eating habits is that the high cost of healthy food precludes lower-income households from improving their diet. The research varies on cost; one source claims that healthy foods are too expensive,[64] another source claims that healthy foods (other than fresh produce) are 8 percent cheaper than unhealthy foods,[65] and another source claims that the "healthiest" diet costs about $1.50 more a day than the "least" healthy diet (the cost of less than two packs of cigarettes per week).[66] The cost of food does not seem to be a leading factor in eating habits, and neither are food deserts. All income classes in the United States are within commuting distance to healthy foods. In 2015, the median distance to the nearest food store for the overall U S population was 0.9 miles, the longest commute being 3.1 miles for the average rural shopper.[67] People living below the federal poverty line predominately live in cities and associated suburbs where the commutes to grocery stores are shorter with more access to public transportation.[68] Ecommerce has also reduced geographic food inequality by providing online grocery shopping.

Using a structural demand model, it was found that exposing low-income households to the same products and prices available to high-income households reduces nutritional inequality by only 9 percent, while the remaining 91 percent is driven by differences in demand.[69] Distance and the cost variation between refined foods and nutritious whole foods is not enough to deter low-income households from improving their diet. Therefore, the primary cause(s) of the stark differences in eating behavior must be found in the individual.

Education, allergy addictions, upbringing, and the gut's microbiome can all be accountable for establishing a person's eating preferences. The conclusion many researchers arrive at when studying the discrepancies in eating habits is that there is a lack of education. Alcoholism was used to illustrate allergy addictions, but this can also apply to food. Much of the food in grocery stores has scads of synthetic ingredients, including chemical dyes, preservatives, and artificial sweeteners and flavors. There are also chemicals in food that are not on the ingredient list, like glyphosate and pesticides. Many of these chemicals have the potential to cause an allergic addiction. It is ironic that the foods and chemicals that people crave are poisons. No one has ever been addicted to vegetables the way people can crave processed food.

The food people are addicted to has an emotional component. Thinking about eating and the moments after eating can cause hypoeuphoria, followed by a hangover and depression. The earlier people are introduced to addictive processed foods, the harder it is to overcome the addiction. Uneducated parents pass on their own addictive eating behavior to their children, not knowing the damage it can do to their bodies. The body adapts to repetition, so when someone attempts to change a long-standing diet, the body revolts in a biochemical backlash. Sudden changes to a diet, especially a highly addictive diet, can cause clinical depression, detox symptoms, apathy, and anxiety. Likewise, a person who never eats processed foods can suffer stomach discomfort and possibly agitation, anger, fatigue, and headaches if they start eating them. The foods people eat become intrinsic to the individual because they influence gene expression, the presumed center of a person's individuality. For these reasons the body and personality need time to acquiesce to a new diet. Therefore, making small, incremental changes is the safest and most sustainable way to permanently alter an eating lifestyle.

Behavior and the Microbiome

The dramatic changes a person experiences when changing their diet are partly due to their microbiome, the bacteria and single-celled organisms that take up residency in the body. A person's microbiome is as unique as their fingerprints and has a powerful influence on diet, mood, and behavior. There are trillions of bacteria living in the large intestine and billions living in the small intestine. Bacteria and single-celled organisms are also found in the urinary tract, genital tract, upper respiratory tract, oral cavity, eyes, and skin.

Sites containing a well-established microbiome include the following:

Skin:
- Bacteria: *Staphylococcus, Micrococcus, Corynebacterium, Propionibacterium, Mycobacterium*
- Fungi: *Malassezia* yeast
- Arthropod: *Demodex* mite

Oral cavity:
- Bacteria: *Streptococcus, Neisseria, Veillonella, Staphylococcus, Fusobacterium, Lactobacillus, Bacteroides, Corynebacterium, Actinomyces, Eikenella, Treponema, Haemophilus*
- Fungi: *Candida*
- Protozoa: *Trichomonas tenax, Entamoeba gingivalis*

Large intestine and rectum:
- Bacteria: *Bacteroides, Fusobacterium, Eubacterium, Bifidobacterium, Clostridium,* fecal *Streptococci, Peptococcus, Lactobacillus,* coliforms
- Fungi: *Candida*
- Protozoa: *Entamoeba coli, Pentatrichomonas hominis*

Upper respiratory tract:
- Microbial populations exist in the nasal passages, throat, and pharynx owing to their proximity; the microbiome in the respiratory tract is similar to that of the oral cavity.

Genital tract:
- Bacteria: *Lactobacillus, Streptococcus, Corynebacterium, Escherichia, Mycobacterium*

Urinary Tract:
- Bacteria: *Staphylococcus, Streptococcus,* coliforms
- Fungi: *Candida*[70]

Collectively, the bacteria and other organisms living on and in an adult's the body weigh about five pounds, which is roughly the same weight as the brain. There are close to ten times the number of bacteria cells in the human body as there are human cells. If the human body was a democracy, then bacteria would have the voting majority in decision-making.

Many of the bacteria that colonize a person's body come from his or her mother. Streptococci, staphylococci, and lactobacilli are passed from the mother's vagina to the child during birth.[71] The Bifidobacterium acquired from breast milk colonizes the newborn's large intestine, where it protects the child from intestinal pathogens by converting sugars to lactic acid. Newborns that are bottle-fed are likely to have their large intestines colonized by lactobacilli, enteric streptococci, and staphylococci.[72] The most influential and essential bacteria in the body are inherited maternally and live in the human mammalian cell.

Mitochondria

Greek for thread (*mito*) and granule (*chondria*).

Mammalian cells are eukaryotic. Bacteria cells are prokaryotic. Eukaryotic cells have small, isolated compartments called organelles. Each organelle has a different function that supports the cell's health. The mitochondria are organelles passed down from the mother. They are gram-negative bacillus (rod-shaped) bacteria wrapped in a eukaryotic membrane.[73]

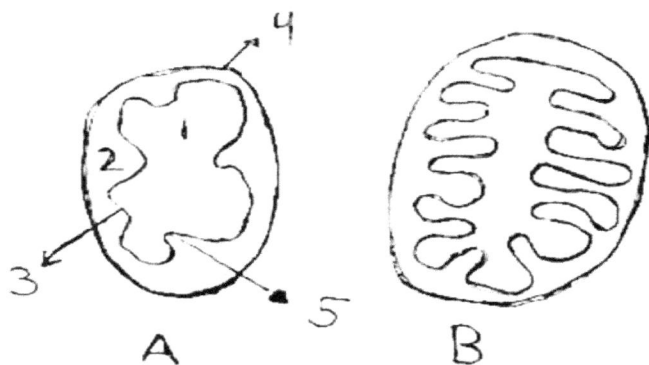

Figures A and B both show mitochondria. Figure A is a mitochondrion that is relatively undeveloped compared with figure B. Mitochondria can range in weight from 0.5 to 1 microgram. The heart and skeletal muscles have large, developed mitochondria because they use more oxygen and require more energy. The mitochondria in liver cells are less developed. Other than erythrocytes (red blood cells), all human cells have mitochondria.

Anatomy of a Mitochondrion:
1. The matrix has a pH of 7.8. It is less than 50 percent water, with a gel-like consistency. The citric acid cycle is located in the matrix.
2. The intermembrane space has a pH between 7.0 and 7.4.
3. The inner membrane is the gram-negative bacterial membrane. It is roughly 75 percent protein, which is common for bacterial membranes.
4. The outer membrane is mammalian, or eukaryotic. It is roughly 52 percent protein, which is common for other eukaryotic membranes. The outer membrane has open passages called porins that are ten kilodaltons wide. Porins allow small chemicals like ATP (energy), citrate, and small proteins to freely pass between the mitochondria and the rest of the cell.
5. Cristea are invaginations, or folds, of the inner membrane.

The eukaryotic cells that make up the human body once lived in a limited-oxygen, or anaerobic, environment. During the Siderian period (2.46–2.426 billion years ago), the oxygen levels on Earth began to rise. This was known as the oxygen revolution or oxygen crisis. The rise in atmospheric oxygen led to a mass extinction of anaerobic organisms.[74] It was during this transition in Earth's atmosphere that the mammalian eukaryotic cells absorbed the gram-negative aerobic bacteria that are now known as mitochondria. The mitochondria are one of the only aerobic areas in the cell and require oxygen to function properly. The body uses iodine, glutathione, and iron to deliver oxygen to the mitochondria.[75]

Each human cell can have up to two thousand mitochondria, making up 20 percent of the cell by volume.[76] Mitochondria have their own life cycles and genes. The evolutionary symbiotic relationship between the mitochondria and mammalian cells is responsible for life as we know it today. Mitochondria use sugar and oxygen to supply the body with the energy molecule adenosine triphosphate (ATP).

GLUCOSE + OXYGEN → CARBON DIOXIDE + WATER + ATP

This process is known as cellular respiration and is carried out in part through the citric acid cycle. It also produces carbon dioxide and water; both are needed to make hydrochloric acid for the stomach to break down proteins and sodium bicarbonate to keep the blood pH alkaline. The mitochondria can also convert fat and protein into ATP or reverse the process to synthesize fats, proteins, and carbohydrates, which the body can use to make new cells and tissue.[77] Mitochondria are essential for apoptosis, or programmed cell death. When cells die through apoptosis, they release critical nutrients and building blocks to neighboring cells, improving the health of the tissue. Cells that do not die correctly can damage neighboring tissue, cause inflammation, and lead to cancer.[78]

To keep the mitochondria healthy and functioning properly, several vitamins and minerals are necessary. The mitochondria and mammalian cells have their own superoxide dismutase, a powerful antioxidant. The superoxide dismutase synthesized by mammalian cells requires copper and zinc as cofactors, while the one synthesized by the mitochondria requires manganese as a cofactor. Niacin (vitamin B3), pantothenic acid (vitamin B5), riboflavin (vitamin B2), CoQ10, biotin (vitamin B7), copper, thirty-three atoms of sulfur, and twenty-seven atoms of iron are used to convert glucose to ATP.[79] Dietary sulfur comes primarily from protein, specifically cysteine.

Exercise directly stimulates the development of mitochondria. People who exercise regularly may have mitochondria double the size of an indolent person's. This dramatically increases the surface area of the inner membrane by generating more cristea, or membrane folds. The inner membrane is where most of the energy is produced in the mitochondria and where CoQ10 and most of the iron and sulfur are used. The increased demand for energy from exercise raises the demand for sulfur and iron. As a result, athletes are more likely to experience an iron deficiency and anemia.[80] The way exercise and diet affect the mitochondria is another example of how people can willfully change their chemistry with focused effort. Mitochondria are essential to life. However, the bacteria living throughout a person's digestive system and on the body can vary with lifestyle and diet.

There are four types of bacteria living in the body: beneficial, commensal, opportunistic, and pathogenic. Beneficial bacteria help with peristalsis (the physical motion that moves food through the digestive system) and produce several vitamins, including B1, B2, B3, B5, B6, B9, B12, A, and K2. They also turn fatty acids into energy and produce lactic acid, which helps prevent the overgrowth of pathogenic bacteria and yeast. Lactic acid also aids in the digestion and absorption of minerals like magnesium, calcium, manganese, copper, and iron.

Beneficial bacteria produce many of the neurotransmitters found in the brain, like serotonin, dopamine, GABA, acetylcholine, and melatonin. Commensal bacteria, from the host's perspective, are neither harmful nor beneficial. These bacteria take up space, which helps prevent harmful organisms from colonizing. However, if the host gets sick, commensal bacteria can become parasitic. Opportunistic bacteria are more harmful than commensal bacteria and usually cause a secondary infection when someone is sick. Infections from opportunistic pathogens are common in hospital settings and in people with low-functioning immune systems. Pathogenic bacteria are more virulent than opportunistic bacteria and are more likely to cause disease in healthy people.[81]

Bacteria directly influence mood, behavior, and IQ. Researchers determine a mouse's mood by measuring the length of time it will swim before giving up. When mice that were labeled as depressed were fed the probiotic *Lactobacillus* JB-9, they swam longer, their stress hormone levels dropped, and their memory and IQ scores improved.[82] Mice were also used as research models to connect personality and gut bacteria. The mice were separated into two groups based on personality. One group was timid and docile, while the other group was gregarious and exploratory. The researchers killed their gut bacteria with antibiotics and then fed the mice the bacteria that were common among the other group. As a result, the timid and docile mice became exploratory and gregarious, while the gregarious and exploratory mice became docile and timid.[83]

Bacteria's ability to have a powerful effect on mood, behavior, and health is due in part to the vagus nerve. Known as the wandering nerve, the vagus nerve connects the brain, throat, heart, lungs, liver, pancreas, gut, duodenum, and descending colon. The vagus nerve is also bidirectional, sending messages to and from the brain, heart, lungs, liver, and gut. The gut connects to the brain's emotional, cognitive areas via the vagus nerve.[84] As a result of this bidirectional connection, a person's emotional state affects gut function; when a person is stressed, it will cause gut dysfunction. Likewise, gut function affects a person's emotional state, behavior, and intelligence. The mice that were fed *Lactobacillus* JB-9 lost their benefits when the vagus nerve connecting the gut to the brain was cut.[85] Gut bacteria may produce a vibration that travels along the vagus nerve, creating some of these benefits. Doctors can induce anxiety or calm a person down by stimulating the vagus nerve. The mood a patient feels is based on the frequency or vibration the doctor uses.

Gut Dysbiosis

Gut dysbiosis is caused by a disruption to the microbiome, resulting in an imbalanced microbiota.

There are three types of dysbiosis:
1. The loss of good bacteria from the gut.
2. The overgrowth of harmful bacteria in the stomach and digestive tract.
3. The loss of microbiome diversity.

It is common for someone to suffer from all three types of gut dysbiosis with varying symptoms, including diarrhea, constipation, chronic fatigue, digestive problems, trouble urinating, acid reflux or heartburn, vaginal or rectal infections and/or itching, food intolerances, gas and bloating, inflammation and aching joints, acne, skin rashes and psoriasis, ADHD, anxiety, and depression.[86]

Some causes of gut dysbiosis include:
1. Sudden dietary changes.
2. Accidental consumption of chemicals such as lingering pesticides on unwashed fruit.
3. Drinking two or more alcoholic beverages per day.
4. New medications, such as antibiotics, that affect the gut flora.
5. Poor dental hygiene, which allows bacteria to grow out of balance in the mouth.
6. High levels of stress or anxiety that weaken the immune system.
7. Harmful bacteria from unprotected sex.[87]

The overgrowth of harmful bacteria or yeast is recognized as one of the main causes of dysbiosis. However, the overgrowth of any bacteria or gut resident has the potential to induce an imbalanced microbiome that can lead to gut dysbiosis. *Escherichia coli* (*E. coli*) is a natural resident of the digestive tract that produces vitamin K and a protein that helps break down salmonella and shigella.[88] Species of the fungus *Candida* are also natural residents of the body that aid in digestion and nutrient absorption. When these organisms are a balanced part of the microbiome, they promote a healthy digestive tract. Diets that introduce more of these organisms to the digestive system or diets that kill other residents native to the body put the individual at risk of dysbiosis. A healthy digestive system is predicated on a balanced, varied microbiota that prevents any one native species from overgrowing or dying off.

The American diet is centered on an organism foreign to the microbiome. *Saccharomyces cerevisiae* is the yeast used to make beer, wine, and bread. It is part of a fungal family that includes many plant and human pathogens as well as the fungus that produces penicillin.[89] Fungal infections have dramatically increased in developed countries over the last century. *Saccharomyces cerevisiae* has been connected to a wide variety of infections and is now recognized as an emerging fungal pathogen.[90] Doctors also use *S. cerevisiae* as an antibiotic to treat diarrhea.

It naturally produces a potent, broad-range, antimicrobial, low-weight protein (peptide) called saccharomycin. This antimicrobial peptide indiscriminately kills bacteria, viruses, and fungi.[91] Habitually eating foods containing one specific organism poses the risk of dysbiosis by interfering with the balanced diversity in the digestive tract. Organisms like *S. cerevisiae* threaten the natural residents of the body and the mitochondria by releasing low-weight, broad-spectrum antimicrobial chemicals. Small peptides like saccharomycin and antibiotics are able to passively enter the outer membrane of the mitochondria through porins and potentially kill these essential gram-negative bacteria.

Once the gut becomes dysbiotic, digesting and absorbing nutrients, fats, carbohydrates, and proteins from food is affected. The overgrowth and dying off of organisms central to a healthy microbiome can also lower the production of essential vitamins. Dysbiosis can also reduce the production of lactic acid, diminishing the body's ability to absorb critical metals and minerals from food. Gut dysbiosis can also elevate beta alanine levels. Beta alanine is a nonessential amino acid. Bacteria synthesize beta alanine to make pantothenic acid (B5) and coenzyme A.[92] The body requires pantothenic acid and coenzyme A to make ATP, the primary energy molecule. Although beta alanine is necessary for proper health, elevated levels are a biomarker of food allergies and asthma, a staphylococcus or streptococcus infection, or a yeast or fungus infection.[93] The breakdown of damaged tissue and tumors also increases beta alanine levels. Beta alanine and taurine, another nonessential amino acid, compete for reabsorption in the kidneys. The overproduction of beta alanine can lead to kidney dysfunction and a taurine deficiency.[94]

Taurine

Taurine is the most abundant amino acid in the body. One of the many functions taurine serves is making bile salt. Bile salts are made in the liver, stored in the gallbladder, and released in the duodenum (the beginning of the small intestine) to break down dietary fat. Taurine has a substantial impact on the GI tract due to its anti-inflammatory and antioxidant properties, which directly affect the microbiome. Bacteria in the digestive tract break down bile salt and use the free taurine as nourishment and to generate energy. Specific strains of bacteria in the gut convert taurine to various sulfur molecules, including sulfides, to protect the body from foreign pathogens. Persistent infection, resident bacteria overgrowth, and diets high in taurine can lead to cancer of the colon when hydrogen sulfides are generated in excess.[95]

Although excess taurine and hydrogen sulfides threaten the health of the body, low taurine levels can be a biomarker of behavior disorders. Autism encompasses a spectrum of symptoms related to gut dysbiosis, including irritability, anxiety, social withdrawal, abdominal pain, constipation, diarrhea, gastroesophageal reflux, bloody stool, vomiting, and gas. Mice have exhibited hallmark symptoms of autism and a 50 percent reduction in taurine after receiving the microbiome of autistic children. Conversely, mice fed taurine showed improved social behaviors and reduced anxiety.[96]

As the most abundant amino acid in the body, taurine plays a critical role in every tissue. It is essential for digesting fats and carbohydrates as well as proper brain development through all stages of life. A taurine deficiency will lead to birth defects of the mitochondria, skeletal muscle, and heart. As an antioxidant, taurine works directly with glutathione to protect the cells and mitochondria from free radicals. The brain, skin, spinal cord, eyes, muscle tissue, and organs specifically have high concentrations of taurine.[97] Taurine levels decline with age. Vegans and vegetarians are often deficient in taurine because seafood and meat are the main dietary sources of the amino acid.[98] The liver, brain, and kidneys can synthesize taurine from cysteine by way of methionine.

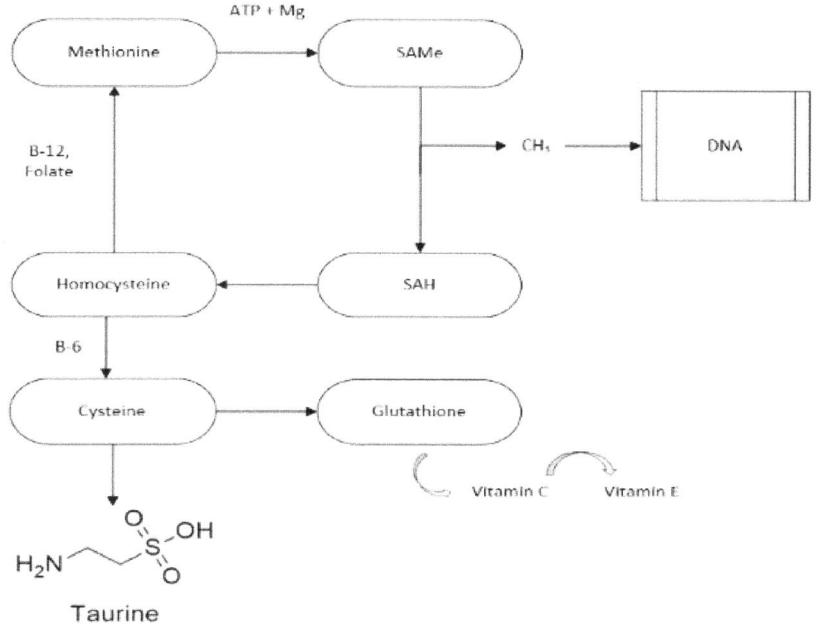

Taurine

Pathway description:

- Methionine → (ATP + Mg) → SAMe → (CH3) → SAH → Homocysteine → (B12, Folate) → Methionine is known as the one-carbon cycle or SAMe cycle. A one-carbon methyl group (CH3) is generated during the process. Methyl groups can bind to genes, silencing them, and protect the genome from foreign pathogens. Methylation patterns across the genome influence behavior and personality. A genome that is persistently under-methylated may lead to cancer. SAMe (S-adenosylmethionine) is vital for repairing genes, expressing genes, synthesizing proteins and neurotransmitters, and digesting fats and minerals.[99]

Paradoxically, the body requires the energy molecule ATP to synthesize SAMe, which is used to make melatonin, the hormone associated with sleep.[100]

- Methionine can be shunted to make taurine and glutathione by way of cysteine. Homocysteine → (B6) → Cysteine → Glutathione + Taurine. Glutathione is a tripeptide made from cysteine, glycine, and glutamic acid. Cells have the same amount of glutathione as glucose, potassium, and cholesterol. Glutathione is critical for removing free radicals, eliminating toxins from the liver, and removing mercury from the body and brain. Many proteins need glutathione to function properly. Glutathione also recycles vitamin E and vitamin C.[101]
- The synthesis of taurine requires methionine and vitamin B6. Both are dietary requirements. Cysteine is a conditionally essential amino acid. When methionine levels are low, cysteine becomes a dietary requirement. Antibodies require cysteine, and all proteins start with methionine.

When the body experiences a taurine deficiency from diet, disease, or gut dysbiosis, it can cause a cascade effect, leading to a deficiency in methionine, SAMe, glutathione, vitamin B6, vitamin E, vitamin C, and cysteine.

CHAPTER 9:
SICK BUILDING SYNDROME

The immune system and microbiota protect the body from foreign viruses, bacteria, and fungi. However, Louis Pasteur believed that disease is caused by a single external organism. Mold and yeast are types of fungus. Fungal cells are like mammalian cells in that they have special compartments called organelles. Yeast cells are white or colorless, single-celled organisms. They do not produce spores and are smooth in appearance. Mold cells come in various colors. They are multicellular, live in dark, damp areas, produce spores, and have a wooly or fuzzy appearance. There are more than fifteen hundred types of yeast and one hundred thousand types of mold. Some types of fungi are dimorphic, which means that they can express characteristics of mold or yeast, depending on their environment.[102]

Saccharomyces cerevisiae and *Candida* (a natural resident of the human body), are types of dimorphic fungi, and both can cause gut dysbiosis. The late Dr. Abram Hoffer, a well-respected psychiatrist, claimed that one-third of the world's population suffers from *Candida* infections. Diseases and imbalances caused by a *Candida* or fungal infection include an impaired immune system; hormone imbalances; impaired thought processes; abdominal bloating; anxiety; constipation; diarrhea; depression; environmental sensitivities; fatigue, feeling worse on damp, muggy days or in moldy places; fuzzy thinking; insomnia; low blood sugar; mood swings; vaginal and bladder infections; ringing in the ears; sensitivities to perfume, cigarettes, or fabric odors; cancer; migraines; Crohn's disease; GERD; chronic fatigue; leukemia; high cholesterol; hypertension; diabetes; infertility; and ADHD.[103] A candida or yeast infection can be caused by birth control pills, steroid medications, NSAIDs, high-sugar diets, and antibiotics. People suffering from a yeast infection are advised to avoid alcohol, sugar, fruit, flour, grains, mushrooms, corn, and peanuts.

Regardless of the climate, fungi are constantly in the air. Mold is essential to life; it breaks down decomposing dead organic material, recycling minerals, vitamins, and amino acids back to the environment. Since pathogens induce decay, it is possible that mold acts as a vector by storing pathogens and viruses as they break down dead tissue. Preventing toxic mold and other pathogenic organisms from colonizing the home is necessary for maintaining health. There are many natural residents in the human body that can become pathogenic if the body becomes sick. There are also pathogenic organisms in the environment that will make people sick if they are ingested in large enough quantities. *Penicillium*, *Aspergillus*, *Cladosporium*, and *Stachybotrys* (black mold) are different types of mold that will make people sick if they are allowed to grow unchecked in the home. Symptoms common to mold disease are headaches, fatigue, skin rashes, diarrhea, allergies, immune suppression, flu-like reactions, sore throat, liver dysfunction, body aches and pains, weight loss, depression, chronic cough, shortness of breath, and cancer.

The whole spectrum of symptoms a person can have from a mold infection is often referred to as "sick building syndrome." Reports of sick building syndrome are on the rise. It is usually caused by water damage in the walls and ceiling or coming in contact with any building material that can act as a substrate or growing source for mold and fungi. Correcting moisture problems, removing any mold-infested material, and decontaminating the living space are the common courses of action when dealing with a mold outbreak. People living in valleys and damp areas are more likely to have issues with mold.

Mold can be an occupational hazard as well; farmer's lung, tea picker's lung, bagassosis (from inhaling cane sugar fibers), and bark stripper's lung (from inhaling fungal spores while stripping bark from maple logs) are all caused by mold. Mold can spread quickly, especially if the growing conditions are right. One mold colony can have up to five thousand spore-bearing structures, and each spore structure can have up to two thousand spores. Keeping the immune system healthy and the mold populations down through routine cleaning and proper drainage is the best approach to preventing sick building syndrome. There are scads of cleaning products available, with varying efficacies.

Cleaning Products

Following proper PPE (personal protective equipment) guidance will minimize the potential harmful side effects cleaning products can have on the user.

- Iodine is effective against all classes of microorganisms it comes in contact with.
- Chlorine kills bacterial cells, endospores, fungi, and viruses.
- Chlorhexidine kills bacteria, with varying effect on viruses and fungi (does not kill spores).
- Ethanol (grain) is a 70–95 percent solution used in skin detergents. It does not kill bacterial spores but can kill tubercle bacilli and fungal spores, with mixed effectiveness on viruses. Seventy percent solutions are more effective than 100 percent.
- Silver (colloidal) is a mild germicide that is safe to use in rinses for the mouth, eye, nose, and vagina.
- Phenols are a strong microbicide. They will kill bacteria, fungi, and most viruses. The most common phenol is triclosan; it is the active ingredient in Lysol and is common in hand soap.
- Hydrogen peroxide kills bacteria, viruses, and fungi (not spores).
- Soaps are weak antimicrobials.[104]

A mold or yeast infection is often recognized as a secondary infection. One-quarter of all hospital infections are caused by candida. Developing a healthy lifestyle and including foods that maintain beneficial candida and yeast populations will minimize the potential of a harmful secondary infection. Out of the one hundred thousand species of fungi, only three hundred have been linked to animal disease. Plants have developed a wide variety of antimicrobial and antifungal chemicals since they are significantly more threatened by fungi than animals. Organic herbs and vegetables common to a healthy diet may offer internal immune support against foreign pathogens. Many of the essential plant oils are natural broad-spectrum antifungals, antivirals, and antibacterials that can be added to cleaning solutions for increased efficacy.

CHAPTER 10:
ZOONOTIC DISEASE

P ets can transmit diseases to their owners. Based on the National Pet Owners Survey, roughly 70 percent of families, or 90.5 million families, living in the United States owned a pet in 2021–2022, with 69 million families owning one or more dogs and 45.3 million families owning one or more cats.[105] Dogs and cats are significant reservoirs for zoonotic infections. Pets can transmit viral, parasitic, and bacterial diseases to humans. Pathogens from pets can be transmitted through saliva, aerosolized body fluids, contaminated urine or feces, and direct contact with the animal. Changes in mental health and behavior can be caused by any zoonotic infection in addition to the common symptoms associated with the disease.

Toxoplasma gondii is a single-celled organism that lives in the stomachs of cats. More than 40 million men, women, and children carry the *Toxoplasma* parasite.[106] Rats infected by the parasite are compulsively attracted to cats and cat urine. The parasite suppresses the rat's instinct to avoid cats to improve its chances of returning to a cat's stomach. This parasite's ability to replace instinctual fear with affection is suicidal for the rats and symbiotic for the cats. Moreover, a rat does not regain its instinctual fear of cat urine or cats even after the infection is cleared from its system, suggesting that toxoplasmosis causes permanent behavioral changes.[107] People with this infection are more likely to suffer from car accidents; exhibit reckless behavior; develop schizophrenia, depression, and anxiety; and have an altered response to cat urine.

The parasite changes human behavior in part by interfering with serotonin and dopamine levels, growing cysts in the brain, and changing a person's relationship to fear by altering the function of their amygdala.[108] *Toxoplasma gondii* is a parasite and is not considered part of a human's microbiome. However, its ability to change a host's behavior is a clear and disturbing example of the impact viruses, bacteria, fungi, and single-celled organisms can have on a person's life. Toxoplasmosis is a significant threat to pregnant mothers, children, and the immunocompromised. As with all potential pathogens, carriers with a healthy immune system can suppress or prevent the development of the disease.

Zoonotic diseases are extremely common. Scientists estimated that six out of ten known infectious diseases in people can be spread from animals and three out of every four new emerging infectious diseases in people come from animals.[109] These unsettling statistics, coupled with the rise in pet ownership and increased attention to pet welfare, heighten the concern of zoonotic transmission. The global pet-sitting market size was estimated at $1.94 billion in 2021 and is expected to expand to a compound annual growth rate (CAGR) of 11.52 percent from 2022 to 2030. The increased money spent on pet care includes costs of pet sitting, grooming, boarding, training, and other pet services.[110] As these social enrichments become more common, the chance of spreading diseases between pets and owners rises. Once a pet becomes a vector, it is inimical to its owner.

Known Diseases Spread from Dogs and Cats to Humans[111]

Pathogen	Symptoms in humans
Rabies: A single-stranded RNA virus transmitted by dogs and cats	Agitation, anxiety, confusion, hallucinations, hydrophobia, death
Norovirus: A heterogeneous single-strand RNA virus transmitted by dogs	Vomiting, diarrhea, stomach cramping, fever, chills, headache, muscle aches
Pasteurella: Gram-negative coccobacilli bacteria transmitted by dogs and cats	Meningitis, bone and joint infections, respiratory infections
Salmonella: Anaerobic gram-negative bacilli bacteria transmitted by dogs and cats	Gastroenteritis (inflammation of stomach and intestines), enteric fever or typhoid fever, diarrhea, stomach cramps, headaches
Brucella: Gram-negative bacteria transmitted by dogs	Joint and muscle pain, fever, weight loss, fatigue, stomach pain, cough, night sweats, low back pain
Yersinia enterocolitica: Gram-negative coccobacillus bacteria transmitted by dogs	Watery or bloody diarrhea, appendicitis, fever, abdominal pain
Campylobacter: Gram-negative bacteria transmitted by dogs and cats	Fever, vomiting, bloody diarrhea, abdominal pain, convulsions, seizures

Capnocytophaga: Gram-negative bacteria transmitted by dogs and cats	Sepsis, fever, diarrhea, vomiting, headaches, confusion, muscle, and joint pain
Bordetella bronchiseptica: Gram-negative rod bacteria transmitted by dogs and cats	Pneumonia and upper respiratory tract infection, whooping cough–like symptoms
Coxiella burnetii: Gram-negative bacteria transmitted by dogs	Fever, cough, nausea, fatigue, chills, muscle pain (Q fever)
Leptospira: Aerobic spirochete (spiral-shaped) bacteria transmitted by dogs	Fever, meningitis, headache, cough, musculoskeletal pain, diarrhea, nausea, vomiting, alveolar hemorrhage (bleeding in lungs)
Staphylococcus intermedius: Gram-positive bacteria transmitted by dogs	Cellulitis (skin redness, swelling, and pain) and malodorous discharge (from bite or wound), regional swelling and redness, fever, lymphangitis (swelling of lymph nodes, lymph channels)
Methicillin-resistant Staphylococcus aureus (MRSA): Gram-positive bacteria genetically altered to resist antibiotics; transmitted by cats and dogs	Swelling, redness, red bumps, boils (abscesses) and pain on infected skin, fever

Bartonella henselae (cat scratch disease): Bacteria transmitted by cats	Small, raised solid bumps on skin, lymph node swelling, fever, eye infection, muscle pain
Dipylidium caninum (cat tapeworm): Parasite transmitted by cats and dogs	Anal pruritus (itching), diarrhea, mild abdominal pain, decreased appetite, indigestion
Cryptosporidium: Parasite transmitted by cats	Profuse, watery diarrhea, abdominal cramping, vomiting, nausea
Francisella tularensis: Gram-negative coccobacillus bacteria transmitted by dogs and cats	Fever, ulcers, swollen lymph glands, chills, headache, joint pain, muscle aches, weakness
Toxoplasma gondii: Parasite transmitted by cats	Mild flu-like symptoms, eye disease, brain disease, birth defects
Yersinia pestis (bubonic plague): Gram-negative coccobacillus bacteria transmitted by dogs and cats	Painful, swollen lymph nodes, high fever, chills, headaches, abdominal pain, shock, bleeding in skin and organs; tissue may turn black and die, especially in the fingers, toes, and nose

Several of the zoonotic diseases listed above do not cause illness in pets. The animals either have developed immunity or they become part of the pet's microbiome. The information in the table strongly indicates that many of these pathogens directly target the human's microbiome and digestive system. Any dysfunction in a person's gut will have an impact on their mood, attitude, behavior, and personality. The alterations in personality and behavior may be caused in part by a type of remote transspecies quorum sensing. This type of quorum sensing can cause a pathogen common to a pet's microbiome that infects the owner to augment the person's love for their pet and influence them to remain close to the parasite's natural habitat, the pet's body. A parasite's desire to return to its natural habitat or establish a new habitat in the pet owner may cause changes to their microbiome, chemistry, and behavior. The appetitive nature (bodily needs) of the pathogen may cause the pet owner to waste away as their nutrition is shunted to support the pathogen and their behavior is modified to support its health and life cycle. Zoonotic diseases can develop slowly as persistent low-level malaise with seemingly random flare-ups. Diseases caused by parasites, fungi, opportunistic pathogens, and gut dysbiosis express many of the same symptoms, making isolation of the cause difficult.

CHAPTER 11:
PSYCHOLOGICAL OBSTACLES TO SUCCESS

As sunlight adopts the qualities of colored glass as it passes through it, the desires of the mind are expressed through the body and brain. Persistent, undetected parasitic or viral infections will cause an erosion of character despite the person's intention. The same is true for vitamin and mineral deficiencies. People falsely or unfairly claim responsibility for their behavior, unaware of the hidden compulsions caused by disease, dietary deficiencies, and addiction.

One of the biggest problems people face when trying to recover from drug and alcohol addiction is the belief that they do not deserve a better life. This opinion is created by remorse for past actions. The influence drug addiction has on the decision-making process often leads to self-serving, shortsighted pursuits, at the cost of the people closest to the addict. The shame and guilt that many addicts feel during the recovery process can be too hard to reconcile, causing them to relapse. William Walsh has noticed this sense of guilt as one of the reasons older people are unable to stay on their nutrient and medication programs to overcome behavior disorders. Improving one's life benefits everyone around oneself. Being able to forgive oneself for past inappropriate behavior is a necessary step for recovery and success.

A mother living in poverty can perpetuate her economic status unknowingly during pregnancy. The mother's attitude and attention to the unborn baby can dramatically affect the child's self-opinion after being born. The neural plate, which begins developing in the third week of pregnancy, is critical to the development of the spinal cord and brain. Once the neural plate is formed, the unborn child is susceptible to the mother's mental state during pregnancy. If the mother is stressed about the pregnancy, suffers from a lack of resources because of the pregnancy, or fails to bond with the unborn child, the child is more likely to suffer from a sense of insecurity after being born. An inadequate diet during pregnancy can cause the child to exhibit impatient or impulsive behavior. Dysfunctional relationships, poor financial management, and low self-esteem can be caused by a mother failing to give the fetus proper attention in utero.[112]

Evidence of unhealthy in utero relationships translating into self-esteem and behavior problems may be found in adopted children. Parents who adopt children tend to be well educated and affluent. They also statistically spend more time and offer more educational resources to their adopted child(ren) compared with birth parents. However, kindergarteners and first graders who are adopted get in more conflicts with other classmates and display little interest and enthusiasm about learning, with below-average math and reading assessments.[113]

Children who have trouble adapting to school early in life often face long-term consequences. Researchers found that high literacy scores in kindergarten were positively associated with high school completion by age twenty, whereas low reading and math assessments early in life were negatively correlated with the chances of graduating high school. Similarly, high marks in verbal skills and math from third to fifth grade were positively associated with the level of education reached ten years later.[114] Children's success early in school has a direct and linear effect on their academic careers.

Children that fail to receive stable and secure bonds early in life are likely to suffer both short-term distress and persistent abnormalities in their feelings and behavior toward others. Adopted children are more likely to have had a birth mother who was overwhelmed prior to getting pregnant. The added stress of raising a child would therefore have been burdensome, unwelcome, and possibly embarrassing, depending on the circumstances of conception. The mother's relationship with the inchoate baby can change from acceptance and responsibility to neglect and abandonment the moment she decides to give it up for adoption. The relationship mothers have with their unborn children can be largely overlooked but nevertheless has an impact on the children's self-perception and success.

A mother can also have a positive effect on the child in utero. Pregnant women with a rich support system and a loving partner will likely have a beneficial effect on the unborn child because these women often have an enthusiastic attitude about becoming mothers and can provide their unborn children the diet necessary for proper development. However, it is more likely that the challenging circumstances of poverty and the added strain of pregnancy cause expecting mothers to have negative feelings and thoughts during pregnancy that lead to emotional insecurities and a low self-concept for their children.

Parents are the biggest influence in a person's life. When we are children, our parents are giants, responsible for providing all that is necessary for life. This dependency creates an unmatched relationship between parent and child. From infancy through adolescence, the child absorbs all their parents' beliefs and values like a sponge. Children have higher levels of theta waves, making this process natural. Moreover, children have no frame of reference or contrasting views of the world and society to challenge their parents' perspective. As a consequence, parents can unknowingly or intentionally project their beliefs on their children, perpetuating their role in society. By the time children go to school and begin to make decisions for themselves, they have already agreed to the ideas their parents projected on them.

The Stanford Prison Experiment proves that once a person agrees to be something, they commit to that role. In 1971 the Stanford Prison Experiment was conducted by Professor Philip Zimbardo to determine the psychological effects of becoming a prisoner or a guard and to elucidate how power roles and group identity affect the individual. Twenty-four students were selected for the experiment and arbitrarily separated into either guards or prisoners. Zimbardo created a mock prison environment in the basement of one of the campus halls and provided the guards with wooden truncheons and prison guard outfits. The guards took shifts watching the prisoners and were instructed not to hurt the prisoners or withhold food and drink. The local police "arrested" the prisoners at their homes, charged them with armed robbery, strip-searched them, and had mug shots taken to help authenticate Zimbardo's experiment. The prisoners were confined to prison cells with access to a common area until the end of the study. After only the second day of the experiment, a prisoner blockaded their door, refusing to come out, and on the third day, another prisoner was removed from the study because of an apparent mental breakdown. Meanwhile, the guards in the experiment removed the prisoners' mattresses, attacked them with fire extinguishers, and forced prisoners to repeat their assigned prison numbers to reinforce their identities as prisoners and to harass them. Sanitary conditions declined quickly. The guards forced certain prisoners to urinate and defecate in buckets as a form of punishment. The guards forced some of the prisoners to sleep on concrete floors and be naked as a method of degradation. The experiment was intended to last for two weeks but was discontinued after only six days.[115]

The college students who took part in the Stanford Prison Experiment did so knowing what they were agreeing to. Moreover, these were educated adults capable of making critical decisions who had identities before the experiment. Nevertheless, the students internalized and perpetuated their roles once they agreed to them, even at the cost of their self-respect and moral judgment. This experiment clearly exposed the conditioning people involuntarily succumb to as children, which shapes their self-worth and expectations and determines their role in society as adults. The Stanford Prison Experiment also touched on the psychology of group mentality, creating an us-versus-them attitude between prisoners and guards.

Although group mentality is usually not as stark or defined as in the penal system, it is part of social structures and is sometimes colloquially referred to as the "haves" and "have nots." This class or privilege structure is intangible, existing only in the mind and creating the illusion of limitation. Class structure also falsely presumes restrictions and the belief that the fate of one's life is left to external conditions. Jealousy and resentment become the natural result of this false belief. Ironically, it is these attitudes that actualize the condition.

Jealousy and Self-Pity

The *Merriam-Webster* dictionary defines *jealousy* as follows:
1. Unpleasant fear, suspicion, or resentment arising from mistrust of another
2. Unpleasant suspicion of faithfulness of husband, wife, or lover
3. Grudging envy; as, jealous of rank
4. State or quality of being jealous[116]

Feelings of jealousy are a critical barrier to getting what you want and becoming rich. Even though someone may not verbally express jealousy toward others, the mood is clear from the individual's body language, tone, and attitude. This results in a person pushing away those they are jealous of. Since jealousy is created through resentment of others and wanting what they have, it also pushes the desired object or circumstance away. Staying away from the cause of jealousy is necessary for retaining healthy relationships. This allows the individual to clearly understand what they want and seek associations with those who have it. To feel jealous falsely implies that the jealous individual is not capable of acquiring the desired object or circumstance. It is an expression of helplessness and lack, creating an attitude of self-pity. Everyone has the capacity to make the decisions necessary for acquiring what they want. Objects and opportunity are limitless.

Being possessed by jealousy may reveal the hidden behavior of the individual. Jealousy can imply selfishness since the person who is jealous presumes that the person they are jealous of is unwilling to share their formula for success. This presents a karmic condition; the assumption is that if the jealous individual had the circumstances they desired, they would obstruct others from acquiring the same opportunities. Success for an individual is dependent on the success of the group. Sharing information and resources is essential for survival and prosperity.

You must overcome jealousy and the illusion that others determine whether you can acquire your desired circumstances and objects. You may feel a sense of betrayal and isolation from your confrere as you start to reassociate with reality, as your perceptions and beliefs begin to contrast with the current group mentality. A person's identity is tied to their beliefs and values; by rejecting the group's value system, the person rejects the group, and vice versa. The transition away from poverty thinking may require a social schism to allow you time to reorient yourself to a more accurate or constructive perception of reality. It is best to frame the separation from friends and family who suffer from jealousy as a vacation rather than a goodbye. Spending time alone allows you to shed the impressions of others so that your own desires can emerge. As personal desires develop, writing them down and consciously thinking about them will focus your mind and filter out distractions.

False Associations

Salespeople are trained to use compliments and focus on things they have in common with those they are selling to as a way to sell their product or service. This causes the customer to believe that the salesperson likes them and is therefore trustworthy. Once someone has gained another person's trust, they are able to influence them into sharing their point of view—in this case, the value of the product or service the salesperson is selling.[117] The customer mistakes their feelings for the salesperson as the feelings the salesperson has for them. Buying the product or service is determined by the relationship between two people and the product or service being sold.

Most people like others who are like them. Finding others who share the same opinions and make the same choices diminishes self-doubt and emboldens behavior. People feel comfortable being around others like them because they are predictable, which instills a sense of security and familiarity. Establishing a routine and living in a "safe," predictable environment reduces fear and uncertainty. A narrow routine can also create an echo chamber and contracted thinking. People are naturally biased toward self-affirming decisions. Hiring managers may be inclined to offer jobs to applicants who share the same alma mater or who have the same nationality or ethnicity as themselves rather than the best candidate for the job. The natural instinct to perpetuate their familiar environment may be viewed as racist or prejudiced, when, in fact, they are choosing what they like and what makes them feel safe rather than what they don't like or what is uncommon to them. These biases prevent people from making the "best" decisions based on the needs of the situation, interfere with individual growth, and stoke inequality.

False associations are everywhere in life. Poignant moments do not happen in a vacuum. A bad car accident, getting married, the passing of a loved one, and memories of childhood all create false associations. These strong memories can be invoked and produce elevated emotional responses when a person encounters a trigger. Every time a person passes the location of their bad accident, sees the same type of vehicle, or listens to a song that was playing during the accident, they may have a panic attack or seek to get away from the trigger. Pleasant childhood memories can be stimulated by seeing or smelling the family's favorite meal, hearing pet phrases or childhood songs, or seeing toys from childhood. In both cases the individual creates a false association by linking a similar salient aspect(s) of a previous extreme emotional experience with one in the moment. False associations and fantasy relationships mar objective decision-making, leaving individuals vulnerable to PTSD-type reactions, fear of change, and third-party exploitation. Memory cues can have a positive effect as well. They can strengthen healthy relationships and elevate a person's mood. People make subtle decisions that reinforce their identity daily without knowing it.

The mind seldom focuses on what is happening in the moment. It has an affinity with past events and foreboding potential futures and simply daydreams about scenarios that will never come. As the mind vacillates between a detached stream of consciousness and being present, the chance of linking the two is nearly guaranteed. Shifting focus often links detached thought with external attention, creating phony relationships. A person who internally muses about how much they dislike someone while driving and suddenly gets a flat tire may believe that it's a sign to change their attitude about the person. The mind also inadvertently conflates incorrect associations by connecting two external events happening in the same moment or in sequence. To hear "that is just awful" while looking at a painting will cause the person to evaluate whether the painting is awful or not, even though the statement had nothing to do with the painting. The examples given here are consequences of varied external focus conflated with unrelated thoughts and memories. Conversely, deliberate, intense focus can cause a person to inaccurately associate themselves with the topic. It is common for medical students to believe they are suffering from the disease they are studying. As they learn about the symptoms of a disease, they begin to experience them.[118] The mind's tendency to superimpose its identity on what it is focusing on often creates false associations.

Consciously removing mores and subjectivity from the mind will improve the accuracy and objectivity of in-the-moment decisions by basing them on the current circumstances and relevant information. Practicing this type of self-awareness develops nonattachment, clarity, and objective thinking. The heightened emotional connections to memory cues in the environment will soften as the individual dissolves their false fantasy relationships, giving way to peace of mind.

Everyone's success depends on the success of those around them. The implications of developing an objective, nonattached state of mind in social and business settings are substantial. Hiring the "best" candidate(s) can have a transformative effect for any company. Racial and ethnic divisions will be reduced once people stop pursuing self-affirming circumstances and adopt a more accurate and broader assessment of reality.

CHAPTER 12:

PERCEPTION AND ATTRACTION

Most of the information people use to make decisions is tacit. Our cognitive control of the human brain to make intelligent decisions based on information in the moment is extremely limited. The brain can consciously process only three to four bits of information per second (bps). The visual system, auditory system, reading comprehension, and motor control far exceed the cognitive capacity of the brain; they have a processing power of 4.3×10^6, eight to ten thousand, forty, and ten bps, respectively.[119] The human brain as a whole can unconsciously process 11 million bits of information every second, which causes the brain to take shortcuts in decision-making, often leading to implicit or unconscious bias.[120] Since intelligent cognitive decision-making is not the driving force behind human behavior and selection, then presentation, body chemistry, and inherent programmed instincts must be.

There are several cognitive reasons someone develops an attraction for another person, including proximity, similarity, reciprocity, physical attractiveness, and familiarity. Attraction through proximity is developed by how often someone is close to someone else. People are also attracted to someone who shares similar interests or values. Clear expressions of fondness toward someone will often produce a reciprocal attraction, and physically attractive people will often draw positive attention. Feeling comfortable around someone is another important aspect of attraction.[121]

The way people choose their associations based on their personal experiences and values results in population grouping. Gestalt psychology is devoted to understanding group behavior and perception. Gestalt psychologists have developed several principles or laws that predict perceptual grouping. These include the law of proximity, the law of similarity, and the law of common fate. The law of proximity states that objects close to one another tend to be perceived as a unified group. The law of similarity states that objects similar to one another are perceived as a unified group. The law of common fate states that objects moving together tend to be part of a unified group.

People lack the mental capacity to make unilateral, conscious cognitive decisions. As a result, choices are often made that reaffirm personal behavior and foster feelings of comfort and safety. This makes mimicry a valuable tool for success. Studying the common features and behaviors of individuals who have achieved a desired goal and emulating them will lower an individual's barriers to entry in that group. Dress and parlance are salient distinguishing features of any group, along with common interests, common knowledge, and proximity. For instance, a mechanic, a biologist, and an architect would dress and speak with nuances specific to their professions and pursue knowledge and interests relevant to their fields. If someone dressed like an architect, spoke like an architect, and went to the places architects go, observers would believe that the person is an architect. Public perception enforces the identity of the individual.

People also use subtle and overt body language cues or tells to determine relationships. The cognitive part of the brain, or neocortex, is the deceptive or dishonest part of the brain; it includes Broca's area, which governs speech. The limbic system is where thoughts, feelings, and intentions are expressed honestly. It reacts to environmental stimuli instantly through body language. The limbic system can give off thousands of nonverbal signals that give other people a window into what the person is truly feeling and thinking.[122] The fight or flight response is the limbic system's survival reaction to try to keep the individual safe. In today's society the fight or flight response has devolved into pacifying body impulses to soothe discomfort and low confidence along with postures that connote guilt. Leaning away, shrugging the shoulders toward the head, and physically hiding the body are indicative of guilt. To assuage feelings of discomfort and low confidence, a person may automatically rub the back of their neck, play with a necklace, rub their forehead, or fix a tie.[123] Body language and countenance not only give the subconscious and trained observers an unfiltered view of the person's inner thoughts and desires but may actually cause the witness to mirror the chemistry of the person they are with. When a person sees someone smiling, it automatically activates a reward center in the brain called the orbital frontal cortex, which reinforces and reflects the stimulus (smile) in kind. Therefore, a person's feelings and thoughts could be chemically replicated by those around them. Isopraxism commonly occurs in large groups; people mimic behavior through admiration. It is evident that behavior and thought have a direct chemical effect on the people in a group. Having and projecting positive feelings toward someone will produce a corresponding response. The limbic system communicates the person's desires and feelings through automatic, reflective body gestures.

It takes one-tenth of a second for someone to gauge how attractive another person is.[124] The subconscious determines our attractions since the brain can only consciously process three to four bits of information per second. The will to survive animates life. It is the motivation that everything else is built on. Being attracted to and having relationships with healthy, attractive people improves an individual's chances of having viable offspring, draws positive attention and opportunities, and improves lifestyle and health through behavior mirroring and group identity. Excluding some cultural and personal nuances, physical attraction is a shared universal perception. Allometry (body proportions), facial symmetry, a slim waistline, broad shoulders (in men), height, hair texture, complexion, movement, scent, and youthfulness are determined by a person's health. These are the same markers used collectively to evaluate whether someone is attractive.

A nutrient deficiency at any point in one's life can be expressed as poor complexion, loss of facial symmetry, weight gain, poor posture, changes in body odor, brittle nails, thinning hair, and low energy. Malnutrition during pregnancy and in early childhood poses the greatest threat to development, success, and survival. A severe iodine deficiency during a mother's pregnancy can cause cretinism in her child, a disease characterized by a goiter, a flat nose, a broad, puffy, dull face, an enlarged tongue, and thick, dry skin and lips. A folic acid deficiency during pregnancy can cause neural tube defects in the child that can be expressed as a hunched back, intellectual disabilities, paralysis, and physical deformities, including a cleft palate. A zinc deficiency in utero can cause skin rashes, truncated growth, neurological damage, and respiratory complications. A vitamin D deficiency in utero can cause rickets, a disease characterized by soft, wide bones, a large forehead, a curved back, oddly shaped ribs and chest bones, and a large abdomen.

Reproduction is critical to survival. Being able to recognize and attract a healthy mate is a hardwired instinct. None of the deformities related to the vitamin and mineral deficiencies mentioned above are considered comely. This indicates that physical attraction is not a subjective opinion but rather the subconscious guiding the individual toward a healthy partner to propagate life through offspring.

Malnourishment is often a forerunner to disease and a lowered immune system. Personal relationships, empathy, and paid professionals provide support for people in poor health. Sick people lose their ability to effectively fight off infections caused by bacteria, mold, and viruses. This raises their susceptibility to secondary infections and increased pathogen load, making them more contagious to people around them. A person's health is revealed by subtle changes in appearance that will naturally produce reactions from other people. In his book *The Liver and Gallbladder Miracle Cleanse*, Andreas Moritz outlines several symptoms the body manifests when it is sick.[125] When the body becomes sick, the skin can become overburdened with acidic waste. If the eliminating organs of the body suffer from prolonged dysfunction, the skin will be flooded with noxious substances, toxins, cell debris, and putrefying proteins. Foreign microbes will colonize around the accumulated debris, causing irritation and inflammation. A person's complexion will suffer from malnourishment by interfering with the natural cell turnover process, leading to drying and cracked skin. When the body is in poor health, the integumentary system will change in response to disease. Moritz has keenly associated different health problems with specific physical changes to the skin as follows:

- A vertical wrinkle between the eyebrows indicates an enlarged and hardened liver and an accumulation of gallstones.
- White or yellow patches between the eyebrows indicate that a cyst or tumor may be developing in the liver.
- Horizontal wrinkles across the bridge of the nose indicate a pancreatic disorder and/or diabetes.
- Oily skin on the forehead indicates poor liver function.

- Puffy, water-filled bags under the eyelids indicate congestion in the digestive and excretory tract, resulting in inadequate lymph drainage from the head.
- A lack of eye luster and shininess indicates that the liver and kidneys are congested and unable to filter blood properly.
- Bad breath and frequent burping indicate undigested, fermenting, or putrefying food in the GI tract. The bacteria that break down food and release gas as a burp can be toxic.
- A nose that is constantly red indicates high blood pressure, an irregular heartbeat, or a heart murmur. A purple nose indicates low blood pressure.
- Eczema, acne, and psoriasis indicate intestinal problems and impure blood.
- Black spots and brown patches on the left or right side of the forehead or between the eyebrows are acid waste deposits caused by gallstones.
- Brown or black spots on the thumb or index finger indicate gallstones stuck in the colon.
- A green or dark temple area at the sides of the head indicates an underactive liver, pancreas, and gallbladder.
- Swollen or expanded lips indicate an intestinal disorder. A swollen lower lip suggests constipation in the colon. A swollen upper lip suggests stomach problems and heartburn.

Malnourishment and disease negatively affect the metrics people use to determine attractiveness. Malnourishment also negatively affects intelligence by impairing the memory and executive functions of the brain. Therefore, attraction and intelligence can have a direct connection. Attractive children have statistically higher test scores and grades.[126] Attractive children also receive more encouragement and attention from their teachers and peers. The social support given to attractive children increases their academic achievement and motivation.

This translates to better grades throughout school and often results in higher-paying careers later in life. Conversely, unattractive children receive less academic encouragement and more negative judgment from their teachers and peers. Teachers are less likely to refer an attractive yet poor-achieving student to a remedial class than an unattractive student with the same academic challenges.

The contrasting public responses to attractive and unattractive people affect their sense of self-worth. Core self-evaluations based on self-esteem, self-efficacy, emotional stability, and self-control create clear demarcations between the two groups. The positive attention that attractive people receive from others results in a high sense of self-worth, while the opposite is found more often among unattractive individuals. The same high self-opinion can also be found in intelligent people. Erudite students receive more psychosocial and instrumental support throughout school. As adults, intelligent people offer society a real functional value and are therefore perceived as more attractive and more likely to procure higher paying careers.[127]

A lack of conformity may account for statistical outliers. Attractive and smart children that undermine or interfere with school mores and teachers' expectation may be met with unfavorable attention. Being defiant or withdrawn from class challenges teachers' values and the teacher's self-worth. The teacher will be tempted to overlook that child and encourage other students who express interest in the curriculum and therefore show that they value the teacher. Showing enthusiasm for the class material satisfies the criteria for attraction. A student who has an eagerness to learn will build a constructive teacher-student relationship. An insouciant or defiant attitude toward academics, regardless of intelligence or physical attractiveness, will cultivate a negative, unattractive opinion from educators and may cause teachers to focus their attention on other self-affirming students. Attitude, physical attractiveness, and aptitude determine the success of the individual.

The brain has reflexes that respond to attractive and unattractive people. Seeing an attractive face stimulates the orbital frontal cortex (OFC), the brain's reward and value center. Attractive people also stimulate the viewer's left hippocampus, a source of long-term memories, which is why attractive people often have a stronger impact on the viewer and tend to leave a lasting impression. Conversely, seeing an unattractive person or situation activates the amygdala and the anterior insula, areas of the brain stimulated by aversive and disgusting scenes. Unattractive people are often evaluated and treated less positively by their peers than their attractive counterparts. However, uncontrollable conditions like blindness elicit more support, empathy, and succor from others, while controllable unattractive qualities such as obesity and facial piercings receive negative emotional reactions. In one study, the largest reactions by the amygdala and left anterior insula (another area of the brain that reacts to unpleasant images) were in response to unattractive faces.[128]

The aversion to unattractive faces may imply that people have control over their appearance. Many nutritional deficiencies and metabolic imbalances can cause asymmetrical bone structure as well as poor complexion. Estrogen and testosterone have a direct impact on an individual's facial expressions and development. Long-term drug or alcohol addiction along with self-neglect will produce a tabescent appearance, and persistent negative thinking can also have a lasting effect on a person's countenance. The parts of the brain responsible for attraction and aversion likely play a role in social learning, which biases an individual to avoid stigmatized peers.[129]

The mental reflex has a similar response to displays of moral beauty. Witnessing acts of compassion and generosity stimulates the orbital frontal cortex along with a diffuse large-scale cortical network that surpasses the brain's response to physical beauty. The brain's augmented response to moral beauty over physical beauty relates to social rules and the effects of group expectations. Processing an act of beauty requires the integration of information received from social norms, which demands more effort from the brain. Sculptures, paintings, architecture, dance, and music also activate the reward center (OFC) of the perceiver, producing the perception of beauty. The amygdala by contrast responds to scenes of mutilation, contamination, and disgust. What an individual finds beautiful or attractive is the product of instinct, self-affirmation, and social acceptance.[130]

Men and women are dimorphic and tend to diverge slightly in what they find attractive. Physical attraction is a significant factor for both sexes but has a stronger draw for men, while women put more emphasis on intelligence and honesty.[131] Survival today requires intelligence more than brawn or brute force, making it the most highly valued commodity for the hunter-gatherer male to have. Women's physical attractiveness is directly related to their health and ability to conceive and raise a healthy child. Some men find women with higher estrogen levels more attractive.[132] Estrogen increases during puberty, which stimulates the development of breasts, hips, and buttocks by raising the production of gynoid fat.[133] Women consistently select pictures of men who have healthier sperm and prefer the scent of men with more facial symmetry.[134] Facial masculinity is correlated with facial symmetry as well as with traits of dominance, another attractive quality sought by women. Masculinity and dominance are attributed to the production of testosterone. The augmentation of testosterone and estrogen induce puberty. Puberty changes and prepares the body to mate.

Having children is one of the primal urges of animals. Therefore, people with elevated sex hormones will likely attract people looking to mate. This is evident from the fact that testosterone and estrogen break down to the pheromones to androstadienone and estratetraenol, respectively. Androstadienone attracts women, and estratetraenol attracts men. When women smell androstadienone, which is primarily released from males' armpits, their mood improves, their focus is heightened so that they can capture emotional information, and their blood pressure, heart rate, and breathing go up, making them more likely to be aroused.[135] More testosterone and estrogen produce more of their pheromone derivatives, making a person more attractive. Female zebra finches that mate with more attractive males deposit higher amounts of testosterone in their eggs. Chicks with higher testosterone beg for food more aggressively, grow faster, and are more likely to become dominant as adults.[136]

The changes a person goes through during puberty result in the urge to mate. This biological process shifts the person's focus and what they're attracted to. Puberty also creates a repulsion instinct in adolescents. To prevent inbreeding and an effete immune system, people are naturally attracted to the body odors of people with dissimilar immune systems. The major histocompatibility complex (MHC) is a group of genes with many different variations that is critical for the immune system. The MHC genes influence body odor and mate choice based on body odor attractiveness.[137] The urge to mate and repulsion toward family members are the individual's biological attempts to have a healthy and attractive child with a robust immune system. Mating outside the family not only increases genetic diversity but also decreases the possibility of having offspring with a lower IQ and a physically dysmorphic appearance (e.g., a prognathous jaw) that is deemed socially unattractive. Seeking a partner to mate with runs counter to the pillars of what people find attractive. Proximity, similarity, reciprocity, and familiarity are cast aside so that a person can find a mate outside the family. The biological changes that happen during puberty cause the individual to sacrifice family security for genetic survival (having a child). The conflict between these forces during puberty can be expressed as oppositional and reckless behavior, confusion, identity crises, depression, and awkward feelings.

Testosterone and estrogen initiate puberty and the urge to mate, but oxytocin may have the largest influence on relationship building and social bonding. The love hormone oxytocin is primarily produced in the hypothalamus, orbital frontal cortex, mammary glands, and uterus. It has a direct role in mating, maternal behavior, and social bonding. Social bonding is a behavior that increases cooperation and develops trust and happiness, which improves the chances of mating. Oxytocin is essential for success because it brings people together. Dysfunctions in the synthesis of oxytocin and its receptor result in symptoms similar to those of autism, isolation, attachment insecurity, and obsessive-compulsive disorder. A rat injected with oxytocin has a calming effect on a cage full of anxious rats.[138] The equanimity that oxytocin produces is expressed as trust for one another, a foundation of social bonding.

Levels of oxytocin spike during coitus, pregnancy, breastfeeding, and physical displays of affection, like cuddling and hugging. The uterus releases 150 times more oxytocin during labor, which helps stimulate uterine contractions.[139] The bonding effect of oxytocin heightens the importance of the mother having direct contact with her child directly after it is born. The mother-child relationship is further developed through breastfeeding. The father will also benefit from the elevated levels of oxytocin released by the mother, as the hormone hedges the stressful period of raising a child by stimulating feelings of love and connection. Moreover, direct contact with the child will raise oxytocin levels in the father as well.

The dramatic chemical changes and shared experiences parents have from dating through childbirth create the foundation for a family. As the child grows up, they express the traits of their parents through appearance, behavioral characteristics, beliefs, speech, diet, and values.

By the time the child reaches puberty, the parents' attraction toward them has become firmly established. This gives the family cohesion as the offspring begins the process of finding a mate to start their own family. Changes in biochemistry in conjunction with the hallmark conditions that define attraction create an unmatched relationship between parent and child. This relationship is necessary for group survival, as it outweighs the obligatory personal sacrifices adults make to raise their helpless children.

CHAPTER 13:
DIVORCE

Marriage is the sacred bond between two people before God. In 1867, 5 percent of marriages ended in divorce, while 50 percent of marriages after 1967 will end in divorce.[140] The steep rise in the divorce rate can be attributed in part to women entering the workforce, the first oral birth control pill, and the "no-fault" divorce law.

The strain of World War II forced women to enter the workforce. The war increased women's employment rates in the United States from 5.1 million (26 percent) to 7.25 million (36 percent). During the war 46 percent of all women between the ages of fourteen and fifty-nine were employed, while 90 percent of able-bodied single women between eighteen and forty were employed.[141] Women proved that they were capable of holding the same jobs as men. Many of the jobs women took during this time were highly skilled and were historically reserved for the opposite sex. Moreover, employers at the time paid women a mere 53 percent of what men earned for the same positions. The increased presence of women in the workforce started to dissolve gender roles in the family. Women were no longer seen as stay-at-home domestic partners of male "market workers." This shift caused a disruption in the interdependent relationship between husband and wife. The domestic partner the husband had relied on was now seeking the same job for lower pay. The cooperative marriage with a clear dichotomy of responsibilities was replaced by a competitive relationship as women left the home for work. Moreover, women gained the independence to remove themselves from unhealthy marriages. During the 1950s and '60s, the baby boomers, who had witnessed this shift in family dynamics, furthered the normalization of women in the workforce as they grew up.

The women who worked during the war saved most of their money (because of the scarcity of goods and services during the war) and were able to help their spouses put down payments on homes. The increased stability and prosperity after World War II gave couples the opportunity to have families. This resulted in a rise in birth rates through the 1950s and 1960s. With the baby and economic boom in the United States came the approval of the first birth control pill in 1960, fueling the "free love" movement during that decade. Retaining their presence in the workplace after World War II, women were offered more freedom with an oral contraceptive. Birth control normalized recreational sex as accepted, encouraged, or inevitable.

Now more married women were working closely with married men other than their husbands, creating opportunities for attraction through similarity, proximity, and familiarity. Working relationships that start innocently can change to coquettish foreplay and lead to the indulgence of uxorious thoughts; however, the risk of conception from these affairs was now mitigated by birth control.

Birth control not only created the opportunity to satisfy appetitive urges but also helped lower the birth rate in the United States. With the opportunity to have fewer children and two incomes, couples had more opportunity to end relationships with less mutual responsibility and financial burden. However, the most significant factor contributing to the increased divorce rate was the introduction of the no-fault law, which replaced the law that required one spouse to bear responsibility for the separation. Once the no-fault divorce law was put in place, the divorce rate rose from 9 to 20 percent.[142] Now someone could have casual sex and get divorced without compunction.

The multiple mating behavior practiced by many animals is done to increase the potential of producing viable offspring. A male sheep will mate with as many females as possible. A male rat will mate with a particular female only once but will mate with as many females as possible. A female chimpanzee will also mate with as many partners as possible in hopes of conceiving. Excessive conception-driven behavior in animals is largely due to lack of opportunity. Scarcity has conditioned animals to capitalize on short-term opportunities for sex and food. Conversely, people have changed their mating behavior because of excess and access rather than dearth, often choosing casual sex and masturbation over the traditional custom of having sex to bear offspring.

During this social transition, the infant mortality rate also dropped by more than 90 percent from 1900 to 1997; life expectancy rose 70.2 percent, from about forty-seven to about seventy-seven; and the US population rose from 76 million to 281 million. Despite the increasing lack of commitment to family, the human population has thrived.

Divorce is the best option when spouses are confronted with irreconcilable differences. However, the gradual social shift toward the acceptance and regularity of divorce has created significant shortcomings for the people involved. The most common reasons for divorce are a lack of commitment, infidelity, and conflict. Infidelity, substance abuse, and domestic violence are often reported as the last straws for ending a marriage.[143] By the age of seventeen, 55.2 percent of children will have witnessed their biological parents get a divorce or separate.[144]

These children adapt and mirror the behavior of their parents, leading to more divorces in the future. The impact divorce has on a child is significant. Having and raising a child is a person's highest obligation. Filing for divorce causes people to shirk that responsibility, conveying to the child that quitting or failure is normal and acceptable. Moreover, it dramatically lowers the child's self-esteem and self-concept. Divorce is often preceded by poor decision-making, shortsightedness, and the inability to solve problems and overcome personal differences. Children of divorce prove that behavior continues to the next generation. Divorce has been shown to diminish a child's future in all areas of life, including family relationships, education, emotional well-being, and future earning power.[145] Children of divorce score significantly lower on measurements of academic achievement, behavioral conduct, psychological adjustment, self-concept, and social relations.

For many, the separation of sex and marriage has turned a holy union into a friable relationship. Children of divorce have a looser perception of family ties, resulting in a greater number of short "love" affairs at younger ages with a greater number of sexual partners. These children often lose their virginity earlier than peers with married parents.[146] Daughters with absent fathers are statistically likely to be sexually active earlier and are more likely to get pregnant as teenagers.[147] Women who engage in premarital sex are significantly more likely to divorce, and women who cohabitate prior to marriage experience a 50 percent increased likelihood of divorce compared with those who don't.[148] The evidence is clear that many children are benighted echoes of their parents' behavior.

CHAPTER 14:

SEX

Sex is an act of commitment and acceptance. The vulnerability, trust, intimacy, and physical act of sex elevates the connection between two people. The feelings generated during intercourse often lead to a long-term healthy relationship and a loving family. However, it can be a cause for divorce. The pageantry that surrounds sex produces a biochemical storm that has an addictive profile like that of street drugs, complete with anticipation, satisfaction, and a two-week hangover. The typical emotional cascade after sex can include restlessness, irritability, dissatisfaction, a desire to be alone, anxiety, fatigue, hostility, fuzzy thinking, cravings, compulsions, and temptations to cheat on one's partner. These feelings can last up to two weeks after orgasm and are sometimes referred to as postorgasmic illness syndrome (POIS), postcoital depression, orgastic impotence, and spermatorrhea.[149] Women involved in successful relatively sexless marriages long-term, validate the serious downside of orgasmic sex. One woman suffered from "inexplicable depression" that lasted for days after sex. Another would "go to the bathroom and cry" after sex despite having a caring husband, wonderful children, and all the money she needed.[150]

The urge to have sex and the difficult feelings that come in its wake can be partly attributed to fluctuations in dopamine and testosterone. Dopamine is a hormone and neurotransmitter made from the amino acids phenylalanine and tyrosine. It is produced in the substantia nigra, ventral tegmental area (VTA), and hypothalamus of the brain. The substantia nigra is involved in movement control, executive functions, and emotional limbic activity. The VTA influences the reward system, motivation, cognition (the process of acquiring knowledge and understanding through thought, experience, and the senses), and the likelihood of drug addiction. It also processes activity from the amygdala, producing an avoidance or fear-conditioning reaction. The hypothalamus connects the nervous system to the endocrine system and controls the anterior pituitary gland, which influences the release of hormones. After a person has an orgasm, the dopamine cells shrink, causing a reduction in dopamine and an alteration in brain chemistry. The VTA is composed primarily of dopamine cells (66 percent) and GABA cells (30 percent). When dopamine cells shrink, GABA becomes the dominant neurotransmitter produced by the VTA, causing the person to experience sudden rushes of anxiety and avoid reward-seeking activities.[151]

Dopamine suppresses prolactin in the hypothalamus. When dopamine levels drop and prolactin levels rise and stay elevated, it can lead to emotional anxiety along with headaches, erectile dysfunction, and low libido.[152] Orgasmic sex causes fluctuations in dopamine levels that produce both the high and low emotions associated with dopamine. When dopamine levels are high, a person experiences cravings, compulsive behavior, delusions, and psychosis. Low levels of dopamine produce depression, sexual dysfunction, low energy, social anxiety, and withdrawal. Roughly two weeks after an orgasm, dopamine levels normalize, and a person is able to experience healthy bonding motivations, increased energy, realistic expectations, and an overall sense of well-being, the emotions common to normal dopamine levels.[153]

Dopamine and testosterone have a direct relationship and share similar attributes regarding personality and behavior. When dopamine levels drop, so does testosterone. Testosterone is primarily made in the testes in men and the adrenals in women. Testosterone and other sex hormones are essential to proper brain function and development; when these sex hormones are scarce, the brain will synthesize them for immediate use. Testosterone influences a person's executive functions by binding to different areas in the brain; these functions include cognitive operations, selective attention, self-control, working memory, cognitive flexibility, and cost-benefit decision-making. For testosterone to influence a tissue or cell, it needs to bind to a testosterone receptor. After orgasmic sex, the testosterone receptors in the reward centers of rats die off and take roughly four days to regrow; during this time, sex and other goal-oriented pursuits become unappealing.[154] Like dopamine, frequent orgasmic sex causes fluctuations in testosterone, leading to a lower overall testosterone level and number of testosterone receptors. Low testosterone can eventually result in reduced gray matter or brain shrinkage and decreased neural activity and connectivity between brain regions. These changes impair a person's executive functions while increasing impulsivity along with emotional instability.[155]

From conception through early development, testosterone is critical for the structural development of several areas of the brain. When testosterone crosses the blood-brain barrier, it can be converted to estradiol (estrogen). Oddly enough, estradiol masculinizes the brain in early development by increasing the density and size of the preoptic area to five times that of females. Estradiol also increases neuronal growth and neurotransmitter synthesis in specific parts of the brain.

This development early in life translates to behavioral characteristics as teens and adults. Researchers claim that the *organizational effect* that endogenous steroids have in early development is permanent. However, after development, the effect that endogenous steroid hormones like testosterone and estradiol have on the brain is reversible or repeatable and is determined by lifestyle and focus. This type of plasticity that sex hormones create in the brain is referred to as the *activation effect*.[156] It has been proved that orgasmic sex directly influences the *activation effect* of steroidal hormones by changing their concentration levels and the number of receptors available to bind to them in the brain, resulting in altered brain chemistry and leading to changes in behavior. People who refrain from orgasmic sex have higher levels of testosterone, which means these people will also have higher dopamine levels as well. Higher endogenous testosterone levels protect the body and brain from all known causes of mortality, including cardiovascular disease and cancer.[157] In 2015, the "normal" level of testosterone for men was between three hundred and one thousand nanograms per deciliter. However, average testosterone levels have been steadily dropping since 1980.[158] The drop in testosterone is likely due to the increase in synthetic materials like phthalates and environmental toxins and a rise in obesity rather than to changes in sexual activity. However, individuals have the freedom to make changes to their lifestyle that raise their testosterone levels naturally, leading to an improvement in mental function and physical health.

Mating

Elevations in dopamine and testosterone produce the urge to seek a mate. When testosterone is converted to estradiol (estrogen) in the brain, it increases the production of oxytocin and oxytocin receptors.[159] Oxytocin reduces anxiety when it binds to the amygdala, removing a potential obstacle in courtship. Oxytocin levels rise during sexual arousal and peak with orgasm.[160] Oxytocin is synthesized in the hypothalamus, where it can be used in neighboring tissues or transported to other parts of the body.[161] From a functional perspective, oxytocin controls the release of milk from the mammary glands and induces uterine contractions, preparing the female for birth and nursing. The vaginal walls are stretched during intercourse, causing the female to release oxytocin. The more the vaginal walls are stretched, the more oxytocin is released, giving credibility to the phrase "size does matter." Massaging the mammary glands and nipples during foreplay will also increase the production of oxytocin in women.

Referred to as the "love" hormone because it is often elevated in people who claim to be falling in love, oxytocin could also be considered the trust, social bonding, risk-taking, maternal, and mating hormone. Oxytocin is essential for normal social bonding behavior, a necessity for survival. A rise in oxytocin lowers inhibition, increasing the risk-taking behavior required by men and women to spend intimate time with a new partner. In this way oxytocin helps induce people to seek sexual partners they are not related to and aids in raising offspring. A female rat and sheep that have their oxytocin blocked have no interest in nurturing their young.[162]

Brain scans have shown that when a man ejaculates, it produces changes in the brain similar to those that heroin addicts experience.[163] The seminal fluid released through ejaculation is replete with various nutrients, cells, and sperm. Seminal fluid also has a high concentration of immune-signaling chemicals called cytokines and myeloid cells.[164] Cytokines are small protein fragments (polypeptides) bound with carbohydrates making them glycoproteins. Myeloid cells are immune cells that remove foreign pathogens from infected, inflamed tissue. Myeloid cells also release cytokines. The overall function of myeloid cells and cytokines is to remove pathogens and sick, dysfunctional cells from the body.

Prostaglandin E2 (PGE2) is one hundred thousand times more concentrated in seminal fluid than the rest of the body.[165] PGE2 is another type of immune chemical that triggers an inflammatory response in damaged tissue, increasing the efficacy of cytokines, myeloid cells, and other immune response chemicals. These immune chemicals and cells released in seminal fluid protect the sperm from being destroyed in the uterus.

The cells and myriad chemicals released with sperm are foreign invaders that initiate a classical inflammation response in the cervix, similar to what would happen if a person were fighting off a foreign pathogen, experiencing kidney rejection, or removing dead or dysfunctional cells.

The changes to the cervix and uterus from seminal fluid include the following:
1. Inflammation or increased blood supply to tissue (cervix).
2. Increased capillary permeability to allow larger immune molecules from blood to the infected area.
3. The migration of immune cells to the infected area (cervix).[166]

Cytokines, myeloid cells, PGE2, and other substances from semen that increase immunity intensify the inflammation response of the cervix.

The chemical reaction that is generated during intercourse and ejaculation is necessary for the proper development of the child. If some of these inflammatory chemicals or other substances are missing during conception, the child is at risk of developing several metabolic dysfunctions and increased fat accumulation. Many of the substances in semen are there to protect the sperm and ensure conception; these substances include the antioxidants catalase, vitamin C, and superoxide dismutase (SOD). Seminal fluid changes the environment's pH to protect sperm. The pH of semen is 8, making it a strong base; the pH of the vagina is between 3.8 and 4.5, and the pH of the cervix is 6.5.[167] The sperm would die if they were released in an acidic environment, which is why they are protected in a strong basic fluid.

The chemical storm that happens during sex dramatically changes the cervix, preparing the woman for pregnancy. Having sex on birth control prevents conception, but not the dramatic immune reaction and environmental changes that come with it. The vagina maintains its acidic pH to prevent the growth of foreign pathogens and local dysbiosis. The strong alkaline buffering pH that protects sperm will raise the vaginal pH, giving foreign pathogens that were inhibited from growing the ability to colonize and infect the woman. The immune reaction from sex and the foreign cells and immune chemicals from the semen will negatively affect her whole body as she diverts energy, cellular material, and nutrients to replenish her immune system and clear the foreign seminal fluid.

CHAPTER 15:
SEMINAL FLUID

Recovering the substances lost during sex is even more taxing for men. Semen is significantly more concentrated than blood (it has higher osmolarity), creating a drain on the body when it must redirect essential components from other tissues to produce more semen. Moreover, the intense hormone and neurotransmitter changes that happen around sex leave the person with oscillating brain chemistry and an uneven mood for two weeks. When men abstain from ejaculation, the semen is recycled and redirected internally, enriching the body and brain, increasing intelligence and vitality.

Napoleon Hill, Swami Sivananda, Samael Aun Weor, and Ashida Kim espouse celibacy as a means to happiness, vitality, and genius.

According to *Think and Grow Rich* by Napoleon Hill:[168]
- Sexual energy transforms average people into geniuses when sexual thoughts are changed to other thoughts.

- When sexual energy is retained and refocused, it creates individuals with keen imagination, courage, willpower, persistence, and creative power.
- People of high achievement have highly developed sex natures and have transmuted sexual energy.
- Sex transmutation converts a person's sex drive into a superpower for action resulting in genius of their field of choice.

According to the *Ninja Book of Enlightenment* by Ashida Kim:[169]
- Circulating sexual energy within the body produces higher levels of understanding of self and others and promotes health and longevity.
- When the sexual energy is activated and moves to upper levels of consciousness, the individual has the urge to mate.
- Withholding ejaculation causes the hormone-rich energized fluid to circulate with the blood and through meridian channels.
- Refined sexual energy turns semen into a clear electromagnetic liquid.
- Refined sexual energy in women results in full, firm breasts.

According to *Practice of Brahmacharya* by Swami Sivananda:[170]
- There is no progress without celibacy.
- When someone is celibate for twelve years, samadhi (see below) becomes automatic, and the person has God realization.
- Celibacy increases one's ability to grasp new concepts, improves memory, and enhances the power of inquiry (drawing information) and clear thinking.
- Celibacy causes seminal energy to flow upward to the brain, where it is stored as Ojas (spiritual energy).
- Ojas is used for contemplation.

- When Ojas is stored in the brain, the person becomes very intelligent and has a magnetic aura and lustrous eyes. They can easily influence other people and have attractive, awe-inspiring personalities.
- Ojas gives a person the ability to perform tremendous amounts of mental work.
- Celibacy will change the scent of the person from that of a buck goat to that of a lotus.
- Eventually, the body will stop making semen.

According to *The Perfect Matrimony* by Samael Aun Weor:[171]
- Sexual energy has three distinct types: (1) energy for reproduction and physical health, (2) energy for thought, feelings, and willpower, and (3) energy related to the divine spirit of man.
- Sex is the creative function through which the human being is a true god.
- The original sin was the crime of losing or spilling semen.
- Suprasexuality is the process of sex transmutation, which gives the person the power to regenerate the body and brain.
- Sexual energy (kundalini or qi) rises to the brain through the medullar canal along the spinal column.
- When sexual energy is transmuted, it produces a state of ecstasy.
- The sexual sense acts on a molecular level; it is millions of times faster than thought waves.
- Enlightenment is achieved when sexual energy enters and transforms the brain, converting people into masters of samadhi.
- Sexual transmutation activates the pineal gland chakra and the magnetic centers associated with the endocrine glands.
- The endocrine glands become extremely active when refined sexual energy (kundalini) rises through the medullar canal.

- Kundalini dwells in the electrons and is the energy of seminal fluid.
- When kundalini rises through the medullar canal, it activates the endocrine glands along the way. When kundalini connects the pineal gland in the head with the sex glands, the person has profound self-realization.
- When people live correctly, kundalini rises naturally.
- Superwoman and superman are not products of evolution but born from a seed (sperm, ova) used to revolutionize the consciousness.

Samadhi is a state of profound and utterly absorbed contemplation of the absolute that is undisturbed by desire, anger, or any other ego-generated thought or emotion. It is a state of joyful calm, or even of rapture and beatitude, in which one maintains one's full mental alertness and acuity.[172]

Napoleon Hill, Swami Sivananda, Samael Aun Weor, and Ashida Kim came from different faiths and lived in different parts of the world with different cultures during a time when communication was limited. But they experienced the same powerful benefits that celibacy has in the body and brain.

When semen is not used, it is subsumed by the body. Since the authors mentioned above claim that retaining seminal fluid is specifically beneficial to the brain and mental function, the focus on a few of the substances listed below will be centered on how they positively affect brain chemistry.

Here is a partial profile of seminal fluid:

Whole cells: Sperm (four milliliters of semen = 600 million sperm cells), epithelial cells, myeloid cells, endocrine cells.

Protein: Albumin makes up one-third of the more than nine hundred different proteins found in seminal fluid. Amino acids and the powerful antioxidant proteins catalase and superoxide dismutase (SOD) and heparin-binding epidermal growth factor (HB-EGF) are also found in semen.

Ions: Magnesium, potassium, sodium, zinc, calcium, inorganic phosphate.

Vitamins and other molecules: Citrate, pyruvate, fructose, glucose, choline, sialic acid, inositol, spermine, creatine, ascorbic acid, lipid bodies.

Immune chemicals: Transforming growth factor β (TGF-β), interferon gamma, prostaglandin E2 (PGE2), tumor necrosis factor alpha, IL-1b, IL-6, IL-8, IL-10, IL-12.

This list of substances in seminal fluid is not complete. Semen is often high in choline, creatine, and sialic acid and is significantly high in TGF-β, albumin, and PGE2 (PGE2 levels are one hundred thousand times greater in seminal fluid than the rest of the body). The function of these substances will be illustrated below to show that seminal fluid can improve brain composition and mental capacity when it is subsumed by the body.[173]

TGF-β:
- Significantly more concentrated in seminal fluid than in blood.
- Has distinct distributions in the brain, suggesting that it has different neural functions.
- Is found in the cerebral cortex, in the hippocampus, and widely distributed throughout the hypothalamus and amygdala.
- Regulates the growth, differentiation, and survival of several cell types.
- Is involved in the development and plasticity of the nervous system as well as its function in peripheral organs.
- Has been shown to have neuroprotective properties.
- Significantly increases neurogenesis (making new neurons) as well as neuronal regeneration.
- Repairs brain damage by helping to regrow axons and dendritic spines and improving synaptogenesis. Axons and dendrites are parts of a nerve cell. Synaptogenesis is the formation of a synapse, the space between nerve cells where they communicate.[174]

Albumin:
- The most abundant plasma protein. Mainly synthesized in the liver and, to a lesser extent, in the microglial cells of the brain.
- A major component of extracellular fluids, including cerebrospinal fluid (CSF).
- Highly concentrated in CSF relative to other extracellular fluids.
- Has a neuroprotective effect on neuronal and glial cells.
- Removes toxic heavy metals
- Removes heme groups from the brain, preventing the buildup of nitrogen.
- Reduces oxidative stress by acting as an antioxidant.
- Reduces brain swelling and inflammation after injury.

- Repairs and protects the integrity of the blood-brain barrier.
- Removes toxic amyloid plagues that cause Alzheimer's disease from the brain.[175]

PGE2:
PGE2 was first discovered in seminal fluid; it has a specific role in "masculinizing" the brain. Males are found to be more negatively affected by low levels of PGE2 than females.
- Increases the density of the preoptic area (POA) and cerebellum. The cerebellum is larger in males. It is responsible for motor control and integrates sensory information, working memory, and social interaction. The POA is five times larger in males than females. It is critical for mating behavior and regulates sleeping patterns and parenting behavior.
- Directly influences classic boy "rough and tumble" behavior as well as mating behavior during puberty.
- Children, especially boys deficient in PGE2, have a smaller cerebellum and can express behavioral pathology similar to autism.
- Preadolescent male animals with reduced levels of PGE2 develop a smaller, irregular cerebellum, resulting in behavioral abnormalities later in life.
- Increases the number of granule cells in the brain. Males have more granule cells than females. Granule cells are the smallest and most abundant neuron type in the brain. They are involved in processing visual and motor information as well as learning and memory.
- Prevents the overgrowth of nerve cells during development.
- Involved in cell-to-cell communication, mental plasticity, and brain maturation.
- If female rodents are treated with PGE2, they will develop POA density similar to that of males as well as typical male-mounting behavior as adults.[176]

Creatine:
- Particularly abundant in parts of the brain that require the high plasticity needed for learning and memory, such as the cerebellum and hippocampus.
- When dietary creatine levels rise, hippocampal function and cognition are elevated.
- Enhances spatial learning and overall memory, specifically object-recognition memory.
- Increases energy available to the brain and directly influences the expression of plastic-relevant proteins used for learning and memory.
- Supplementing with creatine has improved performance on spatial learning tasks.
- Memory-training exercises increase levels of creatine in the hippocampus.
- Aberrations in the brain's creatine system commonly result in learning and memory impairments.
- Brains deficient in creatine during development are characterized by major mental and developmental disorders, including learning delays, autism, and seizures.[177]

Choline:
- The brain is fully grown by the time a child is age two. Choline levels in the brain are six to seven times higher during this period of development.
- A neuroprotectant and neurocognitive nutrient critical for the normal growth and functioning of the developing brain.
- Involved in neurogenesis, neuronal differentiation (turning stem cells into nerve cells), myelination (adding a fatty protective layer around specific parts of a nerve cell), and

synaptogenesis (forming a synapse or communication gap between nerve cells).
- Along with thiamin (B1) and pantothenic acid (B5), it is needed to make acetylcholine, an essential neurotransmitter for nerve-to-nerve communication and nerve-to-muscle communication.
- Protects and preserves the structure of cell membranes.
- As an acetyl donor, choline influences which genes are turned on and off.
- Acetylcholine is synthesized in the basal forebrain and the mesopontine tegmentum area of the brain. The basal forebrain regulates body temperature, behavioral arousal, and wake-sleep cycles by increasing or decreasing the release of acetylcholine. Damage to the basal forebrain creates an acetylcholine deficiency common in Alzheimer's patients. The mesopontine tegmentum area mediates attention and focus and guides the proper development of the mid- and hindbrain.
- Proper development of the central nervous system requires choline.
- Choline is fifty times more concentrated in the human placenta than in maternal blood. The fetus has a particularly high demand for choline to ensure normal development.
- Optimizing choline levels increase visuospatial memory processing speed and overall infant memory.
- Supplementing with choline reduces cognitive and age-related decline.
- Protects the brain from environmental influences, including alcohol.
- People who practice memory-training exercises increase choline levels in the hippocampus.[178]

Sialic acid:
- The brain has the highest levels of sialic acid in the body.
- The human brain has two to four times more sialic acid than the brains of other animals.
- Eating a diet rich in sialic acid has been shown to increase the levels of sialic acid in neural tissues.
- Plays an important role in proper brain development by influencing cell migration, neurite outgrowth, branching, neuronal pathfinding, regeneration, and synaptic plasticity.
- Lack of sialic acid leads to developmental and behavioral defects in rodents.
- Breast milk contains high levels of sialic acid.
- Animal offspring (rat pups and piglets) that were fed sialic acid learned more quickly and had better memories than their peers.
- Neural membranes have twenty times more sialic acid than other cellular membranes.
- Has an important role in neural transmission, ganglioside (fats found in the gray matter of the brain), and structure in synaptogenesis (the formation of synapses between nerve cells, essential for cell-to-cell communication).
- Increases cell plasticity (structural diversity), essential for neural development, synaptic transmission, cognition, memory formation, and immune function.
- Critical for ensuring proper development of the brain and active plasticity, essential for learning new concepts and responding to environmental changes through adaptations of the nervous system.
- Several studies have shown that the level of sialic acid incorporated into neural tissues increases with learning.

- Learning new concepts increases the level of sialic acid in important memory centers in the brain (the entorhinal, hippocampal, and septal nuclei).[179]

The list of benefits from the six chemicals above is focused on brain health and function. All the substances in seminal fluid are likely pleiotropic (multiple functions), with varying positive effects depending on the tissue or cell. The cache of beneficial chemicals in seminal fluid strongly suggests that it is produced in part to contribute to the maturation and integration of the body. Semen production begins in boys during puberty (at approximately twelve years old), which lasts two to five years. When puberty is over, the male will have experienced all the hallmark changes associated with the process, including a fifty- to sixty-pound weight gain and an average growth of twelve inches. During this time of explosive growth and development, the chemicals in semen, if reabsorbed, would dramatically assist in, and facilitate this rite of passage.

The beginning of semen production and the body's persistent production of semen throughout life suggest that it is critical for internal development and maintenance. Life is efficient at conserving energy. The body adapts to use: lack of exercise causes bone and muscle loss, immunity wanes over time unless the body is reinfected by the pathogen, and the brain dulls when it is not stimulated. Continuously making semen is costly, and ejaculation causes a myriad of unwelcome effects, suggesting that the body is producing semen for a specific internal purpose. Most systems in the body use negative feedback loops to maintain homeostasis; the product of the process is used to turn off the process. For instance, the anterior pituitary gland (in the brain) releases thyroid-stimulating hormone, which causes the thyroid gland to release thyroxine (T4) and triiodothyronine (T3). When T4 or T3 hormones reach the anterior pituitary gland, they shut down the production of thyroid-stimulating hormone, which stops the thyroid gland from releasing T4 and T3.

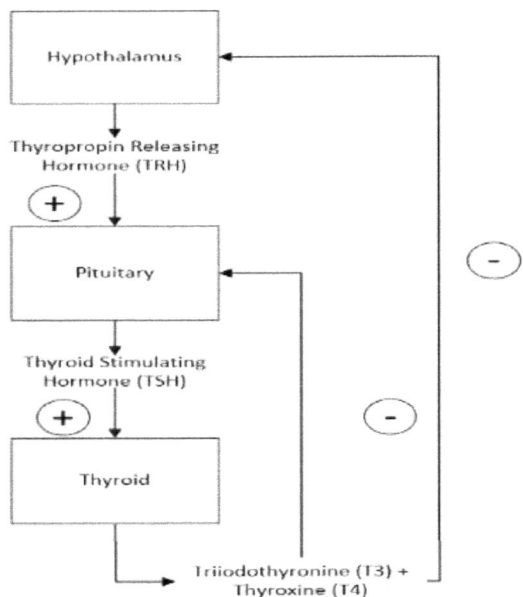

Negative feedback loops like this are necessary for proper health. Swami Sivananda claims that the body will stop making semen when one practices celibacy long enough. Once children reach puberty, the pituitary gland releases follicle-stimulating hormone (FSH) and luteinizing hormone (LH). Together FSH and LH stimulate the production of testosterone in the testes. Testosterone initiates the synthesis of sperm by acting on Sertoli cells. Testosterone is also responsible for the physical and mental transformation that happens during puberty. When testosterone reaches the pituitary gland in the brain, it shuts off the production of LH and FSH, causing a cessation of testosterone and subsequent sperm production.

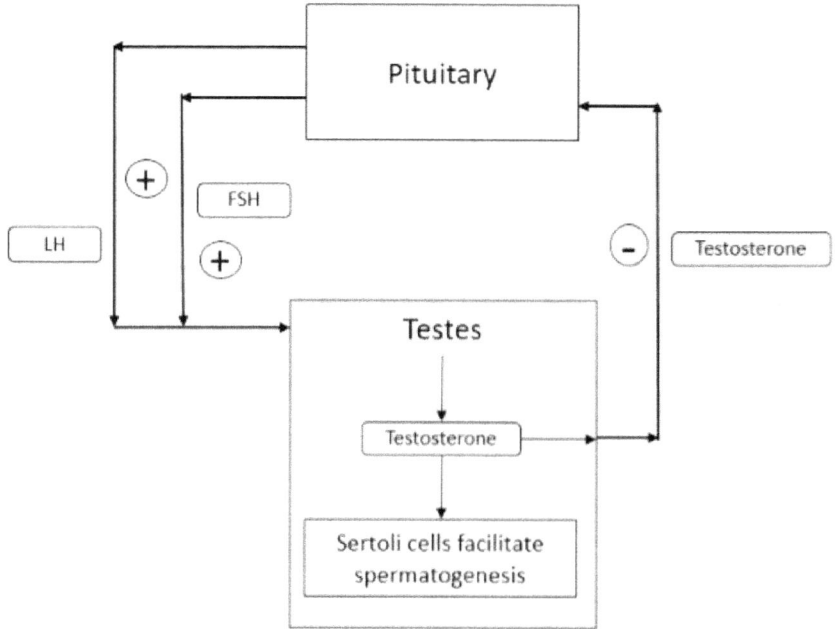

Testosterone and the thyroid hormones regulate the body's circadian rhythm. When light hits the eye, it causes the pituitary gland to release thyroid-stimulating hormone, increasing the production of thyroxine and triiodothyronine from the thyroid gland.[180] Plasma testosterone levels display circadian variations, peaking during sleep and reaching a nadir in late afternoon. The body requires at least three hours of normal sleep to manufacture testosterone.[181]

Testosterone levels and sperm production express the characteristics of negative feedback loop regulation. A hyper- or hypothyroid disorder can result from imbalances in the thyroid hormone's negative feedback loop. Both conditions can produce serious, life-impairing side effects. Having frequent orgasmic sex is liable to disrupt testosterone's natural rhythmic cycle and potentially cause symptoms as challenging as those seen in these thyroid disorders. The fact that men produce sperm for most of their adult lives further indicates that they do not allow the seminal fluid or testosterone to adequately circulate through the body and brain, preventing the completion of the negative feedback loop, truncating maturation. If puberty is a glandular event that drives sexual dimorphism, growth, and the awakening of the reproductive system, then the product of glandular puberty and the awakened reproductive system is used for the maturation of the brain and central nervous system.

The fact that seminal fluid has a pH of 8.0 and a high buffering capacity is further evidence that this precious life-generating solution is manufactured for maturation (a second puberty) and rejuvenation. When a fluid (in this case seminal fluid) has a high buffering capacity, it will retain its pH even when another substance with a different pH is added to it. A pH over 7 (basic) means the fluid has electrons to give; if the fluid is under 7 (acidic), then the fluid will steal or take electrons from the environment. When a body makes new cells, the pH in that area rises to 7.88. The cells of growing, healthy children have a pH of 7.6, while adult cells have a pH of 7.35–7.45. People who are tired, sick, or diagnosed with cancer have a cell pH of about 7.26, 7.18, and 6.48 respectively. The pH of damaged acidic tissue becomes basic during the healing process, as it is making new cells to replace the injured ones. A pH closer to 7.6 is indicative of health and vitality as well as growth and rejuvenation. Therefore, retaining and recirculating seminal fluid with its pH of 8.0 and high buffering capacity will create an electron-rich environment necessary for growth, development, and rejuvenation.[182]

According to the ancient yogic system of health, potency is not just a matter of adequate sexual function. It is that and more. Potency is the inner capacity of a man to project outward—it is his creativity and effectiveness. Potency is based upon many factors—physical, mental and spiritual—and has an impact in each of these realms. One of the most important factors contributing to potency is the presence of a high level of good quality semen in the body. Yogic science teaches that semen is not just sexual fluid for reproduction. It is a lubricant for the brain and the nervous system, like oil in an automobile engine. If your semen is plentiful and "high grade" you will have more resistance to the "heat" of physical and mental pressure than you would otherwise. According to yogic theory, it takes eighty bites of food to produce a drop of blood and eighty drops of blood to produce one drop of semen.[183]

Blood follows focus. When a person exercises a part of their body or brain, circulation to that area increases, bringing nutrition and removing waste. Seminal fluid is concentrated blood used for personal expression. It also circulates in response to focus, delivering powerful chemicals to develop the areas of the body and brain required to fulfill the will of the mind.

CHAPTER 16:
ONANISM

The word *masturbation* is derived from the Latin words *manus*, meaning "hand," and *stuprare*, meaning to "defile."[184] People of all ages masturbate. Infant masturbation, or gratification disorder, is often mistaken by the parents as abdominal pain or a seizure disorder. Children under twenty-seven months masturbate by leaning their pubic region on a firm edge or on the knee of a parent and stiffening their lower extremities in a standing or sitting position. Common gratification disorder symptoms or behaviors also include dystonia (abnormal muscle tone resulting in muscular spasms and abnormal posture), grunting noises, rocking, seeing eidetic imagery (vivid mental images), sweating, cyanosis (bluish discoloration of the skin), lip smacking, staring, shaking, pallor, giggling, and appearing frightened. The habit can also lead to thumb-sucking, phobias, obsessive work, stress disorder, motor tics, separation anxiety, generalized anxiety disorder (GAD), conduct disorder, and oppositional defiant disorder (ODD).[185] Infants can masturbate for as long as an hour or only a minute.

Infants that masturbate have lower levels of estradiol.[186] Estradiol is highest in the brain prenatally and during the first few days after birth, then gradually declines to adult levels. It is critical for proper brain development; it influences gene expression, synaptic patterning, dendrite branching, neuron survival, neuron, and astrocyte (cells that support neurons) differentiation, and calcium function. Estradiol produces permanent changes to the developing brain and acts as a neuroprotective chemical.[187]

Gratification disorders are caused by parental neglect. When parents reinstate affectionate tactile contact, children stop excessive masturbation.[188] Persistently high divorce rates have led to widespread child neglect. Children of divorce are at a higher risk of having their parents unable to provide them normal physical care, emotional support, structure, and discipline. Many children of divorce experience extreme periods of loneliness. Elementary school children with divorced parents have been shown to be aggressive and have lower levels of social and educational competence.[189]

Prolactin levels rise and stay elevated in men and women who masturbate frequently. Prolactin levels also rise in response to psychosocial stress.[190] Prolonged elevated prolactin levels can lead to emotional stress. In rare cases elevated prolactin levels can cause gynecomastia (enlarged breasts) in men. Males who ejaculate frequently are also prone to zinc deficiencies. Nearly a third of all known enzymes in the body require a metal ion (cofactor) so that they can fold and function correctly. Zinc is involved in more than two hundred enzymatic reactions in the body, making it one of the most common metals for these metalloenzymes.[191] Carbonic anhydrase and carboxypeptidase A are zinc-dependent enzymes. Carbonic anhydrase is critical for maintaining an acidic stomach pH and a basic blood pH; it converts carbon dioxide and water to bicarbonate and hydrogen. A dysfunctional carbonic anhydrase enzyme prevents the body from breaking down protein and lowers the pH of the circulatory system. Carboxypeptidase A is released from the pancreas and is also used to break down dietary protein.

Zinc also elevates testosterone levels. Males who abstain from orgasmic sex and masturbation have higher circulating testosterone levels. Testosterone is responsible for the growth and development of tissues and organs that characterize a male, and elevated estrogen leads to secondary sex characteristics in females.

The Biological Effects and Role of Testicular Testosterone in the Human Male[192]

Primary location in the body	Physiological response
Prepuberty	
Accessory sex glands	Wolffian duct differentiation
External genitalia	Growth of scrotum and penis
Puberty	
Skeletal muscle	Body growth (Na^+, K^+, H_2O retention)
Bone formation	Epiphyseal closure (Ca^{2+}, SO_4^{-2}, PO_4^{-3} retention)
Vocal cords	Voice change
Skin	Hair growth (beard, axilla, chest, pubic, and body hair), sebaceous gland growth, and sebum production
Testes	Sertoli cell maturation and androgen-binding protein synthesis, spermatogenesis

External genitalia	Penile and scrotal growth
Accessory sex glands	Prostate gland, seminal vesicle, bulbourethral gland growth and development
Central nervous system	Sexual activity (increased libido)
Hypothalamo-pituitary axis (HPA)	Inhibition of luteinizing hormone (LH) secretion

Suboptimal testosterone levels during puberty can reduce masculine growth metrics. Adolescent males who frequently masturbate jeopardize their development, increasing the chance of becoming a diffident homunculus as an adult.

Internet pornography addiction has the same framework and basic mechanisms as substance addiction. Addiction is an aberration in the brain's reward, motivation, and memory centers. The changes to the brain from addiction have outward pathological, psychological, and spiritual manifestations. Repeated orgasmic masturbation creates biological deficiencies, abnormal mental wiring, and a pathological focus similar to the symptoms of persistent drug use.[193]

People addicted to masturbation and pornography often experience changes similar to those caused by drug addiction. They might:
- become less satisfied with their sex lives;
- engage in risky behavior to watch porn (at work);
- prioritize watching pornography over their responsibilities;
- watch progressively more extreme pornography to feel satisfied;
- often feel frustrated after viewing pornography but continue the behavior;
- become unable to stop watching and masturbating to pornography;

- spend large sums of money on pornography at the expense of daily necessities;
- masturbate to pornography to cope with sadness, anxiety, and insomnia.[194]

Nofap is a growing countercultural movement focused on quitting pornography and masturbation. People on the nofap journey strive to abstain from pornography and masturbation for ninety consecutive days to break the addiction.

Members of the nofap community share similar testimonials, such as the benefits listed below:

No more brain fog	More confidence and positivity
No more anxiety	Better sleep
More active and goal driven	Increased social activity
Increased self-esteem	Increased sex drive
Increased self-control	Deeper voice
Improved body language	More respect from others
Wounds that heal faster	Improved complexion
Increased stamina	More focused
Sharper memory	Increased motivation
Increased muscle growth	Increased testosterone levels

CHAPTER 17:
COITUS RESERVATUS

Biologically, conception is the main purpose of intercourse. The brain chemistry caused by frequent orgasmic sex mirrors that of a drug addict. Coitus reservatus allows connubial relationships to remain strong while avoiding the addictive consequences of orgasmic sex. Coitus reservatus is the practice of having vaginal sex to the point of female, but not male, orgasm. Orgasmic sex is particularly draining for men; refraining from orgasm increases a man's vitality.

Coitus reservatus was practiced and taught by the Taoist prophet Lao Tzu during the sixth century.[195] Lao Tzu believed that preserving one's seminal "essence" or *ching* while a woman has an orgasm during sex strengthens a man's vitality; he absorbs the woman's *ying*. Women are believed to have large reserves of *ying* essence and are less negatively affected by having an orgasm. Lao Tzu also believed that the energy from coitus reservatus was critical for proper brain function.[196]

Intimacy and foreplay increase hormone and neurotransmitter activity. Massaging a woman's breasts and nipples increases her oxytocin and prolactin levels. Vaginal sex also increases a woman's oxytocin, estrogen, progesterone, and luteinizing hormone levels.[197] Both sexes have elevated levels of dopamine and endorphins during sex. Men's testosterone levels spike before and during intercourse. Coitus reservatus also increases production of the pheromones androstadienone and estratetraenol, which make men and women more attractive to the opposite sex. Serotonin is an inhibitory neurotransmitter released after orgasm that blunts sexual urges. Coitus reservatus bypasses the refractory period after orgasm while increasing a healthy, intimate bond between partners and uniformly raises hormone and neurotransmitter levels. Hormones have a cooperative, balancing effect on the individual. When oxytocin levels rise independently of other hormones, an individual can become inappropriately or recklessly trusting. Conversely, if testosterone levels rise independently of other hormones, an individual can become aggressively competitive and antisocial.[198] Coitus reservatus has the potential to elevate hormones and neurotransmitters in coordination with one another, preventing the imbalances caused by addiction.

Moreover, women and men release basic lubricating fluids during sex. Basic fluids are alkaline and share electrons. Kundalini dwells in the electrons of sexual fluid.[199] It is a latent transformative energy coiled at the base of the spine. When kundalini is awakened and circulated through the body and brain, it leads to spiritual liberation. Practicing coitus reservatus has the potential of raising the transformative kundalini energy of both partners, producing an intimate, spiritual, holy matrimony.

Children also benefit from their parents practicing coitus reservatus. Conventional sex can have a cumulative negative effect that produces subtle but significant internal and external conflict between partners. Conversely, coitus reservatus develops a personal connection and improves the health and vitality of both partners. Sex without ejaculation satisfies one's sexual urges, reduces pressure in the reproductive center by initiating the movement of sexual fluid up the spine, and prevents the stressful immune response that women have with conventional sex using birth control.

A couple improves their vitality and intimacy by raising their hormone and neurotransmitter levels concurrently. The electric lubricating fluid released during sex raises the pH and telepathic connection between partners and improves their psychic connection with their children, who naturally have a higher pH than adults. When a woman orgasms, her oxytocin levels spike. Oxytocin lowers corticosterone (stress hormone) and keeps it down for days.[200] Mothers who are chronically depressed have low salivary oxytocin levels. Fathers and children in these households also have low salivary oxytocin levels. Children with low oxytocin are significantly more likely to suffer from anxiety, oppositional defiant disorder, lower empathy, and social withdrawal.[201]

A healthy sex life will improve each partner's perception of their marriage. Men with high testosterone have happier marriages when their perception of their role overload or familial responsibilities is small. Conversely, when men with high testosterone feel that they are overburdened in the relationship, they are less happy with their marriages.[202]

The impact testosterone has on children is determined by their relationship with their parents. Testosterone is related to risky behavior and depression in children when their relationship with their parents is poor. A healthy parent-child connection diminishes the negative behaviors associated with testosterone in children.[203] Children have a higher chance of success when they are raised by parents in a healthy marriage.

CHAPTER 18:
AGING AND PURPOSE

The richest men and women live between 15 and 20 percent longer on average than the poorest men and women in the United States. Wealth has a direct impact on aging and development. Children exposed to the conditions of poverty experience ongoing stress, environmental hazards, family turmoil, violence, divorce, instability, reduced social support, and malnourishment. These factors lead to mental impairments from infancy through adulthood. The longer a child remains in poverty, the greater their mental deficits; executive functions such as planning, impulse control, working memory, and attention are all affected. Children from low-income households also experience slower brain growth during infancy and early childhood. Stunted brain development during infancy often leads to disruptive behavioral problems as young adults.

The brains of young children living in poverty show low levels of electrical activity when they are tasked with exercises specifically targeted to stimulate the frontal lobe; this is evidence that they have rudimentary gray matter. Brain development, specifically the development of gray matter, is influenced by one's environment. Children in low-income families are statistically prone to having lower volumes of total gray matter, particularly in the parietal and frontal lobes. The frontal lobe is responsible for executive functions, while the parietal lobe is responsible for sensory integration, visual attention, and connecting different areas of the brain.[204] Meanwhile, children raised in high-income families have greater resources, more stability, access to better food, and more opportunities for cognitive stimulation and enrichment. A better brain makes better decisions that lead to a longer life. This dichotomy in upbringing leads to a cyclical outcome where the poor remain poor and the rich remain rich.

The reduced gray matter volume commonly found in children living in poverty is caused by a lack of development, not a difference in neuron cell number.[205] The environment offered to children by families with money encourages gray matter maturation; these children have more blood flow, supporting tissue, and neuron connections in their brains.[206] Current research has determined that neurons in the cerebral cortex (frontal lobe) do not replace themselves over time. This permanence may give an individual a sense of identity. Muscle cells of the heart, cells in the inner eye, and DNA also appear to be permanent.[207]

Human DNA is essentially irrelevant when it comes to determining a person's success. There is about 0.1 percent genetic variation between any two people. Moreover, most DNA is currently considered nonfunctional. The human genome consists of repetitive DNA, highly and moderately repetitive DNA, genes with multiple copies, and heterochromatin; all are noncoding genetic sequences often considered "junk DNA." Heterochromatin is sections of condensed chromosomes that lack genes or that have repressed genes. Whole chromosomes, including most of the Y chromosome and one of the X chromosomes, known as a Barr body, can be heterochromatin. Euchromatins are the uncoiled sections of DNA along the chromosome that are used to transcribe and translate into functional proteins. Of the estimated twenty to twenty-five thousand human genes, only 5 percent are functional (code for a protein).[208]

Although the genetic variation among people is miniscule, their environment and diet are fundamental. The time when a gene is "turned on and off" is critical for development, personality, and intelligence. A person's diet is directly involved in how genes are expressed. Certain nutrients and other substances in food can raise methyl groups or acetyl groups in the body. Methyl groups tend to silence genes (turn them off), while acetyl groups increase gene activity (turn them on). The pattern of gene silencing and gene activity is necessary for cell differentiation and development. Infants in utero acquire their own gene-regulating chemical profile, which includes nutrients that either methylate or acetylate genes. If the infant suffers from malnourishment, it may produce a deviant gene-regulating chemical profile, which can lead to abnormal development, disease, lowered IQ, and mental illness early or later in life. The breakdown and digestion of fats, carbohydrates, protein, pantothenic acid (B5), tryptophan, choline, and dimethylaminoethanol (DMEA) can raise the levels of acetyl groups. Folic acid, SAMe, methionine, cysteine, taurine and niacin (B3) can raise the levels of methyl groups. Biotin, phosphates, and zinc also have a direct influence on gene expression.[209]

Other than DNA and the tissues mentioned above, the rest of the body is entirely replaced on a cellular level roughly every seven to ten years. A cell's turnover time depends on its type and location in the body. Some tissue turnover rates are listed in the table below.[210]

Tissue	Replacement time
Rib muscles	15.1 years
Epithelial cells that line the gut	5 days

Epithelial cells in the body	15.9 years
Red blood cells	120 days
Epidermis	2 weeks
Liver cells	300–500 days
Entire skeleton	10 years

The body is constantly turning cells over, replacing old cells with new ones. This process is essential for health and longevity. When old or damaged cells are broken down, either they can be subsumed by the neighboring tissue, supplying them with essential material and nutrition, or the old cells can trigger an immune response, damaging local cells and causing inflammation. When cells die correctly, it is called apoptosis. *Apoptosis* is Greek for "dropping off"; it is programmed cell death. The stages of apoptosis are as follows:

1. Cell volume decreases.
2. The cell membrane breaks away.
3. Chromosomes (DNA) condense.
4. Proteins are broken down into amino acids.
5. DNA is degraded into smaller fragments.
6. The cell sheds tiny membrane-bound apoptotic bodies containing complete organelles.
7. Macrophages (cells of the immune system that absorb and safely process dead cell debris) engage in phagocytosis (digestion) of apoptotic bodies.

Necrosis, derived from the Greek word for "death," happens when a cell(s) dies incorrectly. Damaged or old cells that are unable to enter the apoptotic pathway will damage neighboring cells while causing an immune response. The stages of necrosis are as follows:
1. Cells swell and burst.
2. Organelles swell and burst, releasing harmful fluids into the cytoplasm.
3. Toxins are released into neighboring tissue.
4. The chemical C5a is released from the dying cell to attract immune chemicals to the area to remove toxic waste.
5. Blood flow increases to the area, causing inflammation.
6. Blood vessels to the tissue increase its permeability.
7. Immune cells and immune chemicals from blood migrate to the necrotic tissue.
8. Leucocytes, monocytes, and lymphocytes (immune cells), initiate a complete immune response.[211]

Conditions that lead to a necrotic state are as follows:
1. Physical injury
2. Dramatic temperature change
3. Malnourishment
4. Nerve damage to tissue
5. Bacterial toxins
6. Buildup of nitric oxide and reactive oxygen species (ROS) or free radicals
7. Depletion of oxygen and glucose
8. Viruses
9. Incorrect release of pancreatic enzymes

Sick building syndrome, persistent stress, malnutrition, environmental toxins, living in rookeries or densely populated urban areas, and other common elements of poverty leave developmentally delayed children and their parents more likely to suffer from necrosis.

Financially well-off parents can raise healthy, capable, educated children, and provide them with conditions that enable apoptosis and tissue rejuvenation. Children born in poverty have biochemical challenges in addition to economic hardships, creating a cycle that keeps them in straitened circumstances.

The "I am" consciousness is located in the frontal lobe, one of the areas of the brain specifically affected by poverty. Shrunken, undeveloped gray matter cells common to children living in poverty may be projecting their neglected, malnourished cellular consciousness across the mind of the individual, causing the person to conflate or confuse the message or condition of the neurons as their identity. Poverty begins in the mind and is then translated to the environment. Neighborhoods that were once considered impoverished often experience a gentrification as new families move in and old families move out. As the population changes, so does the group mind of the area; this illustrates that the location of poverty is in part caused by the attitude and behavior of the group. Impecunious circumstances become familiar to people living in poverty, making opportunity and luxury a terra incognita that threatens the comfort of predictability.

The human body is designed to live, grow, and repair itself. People who allow themselves to remain destitute by fostering a low self-concept and villainizing wealth create a direct internal conflict with their own body. The purpose of life should be to get rich. When the mind affixes itself to the idea of getting rich, it echoes the will of nature and unifies the "I am" consciousness with the subconscious. By using the self-programming technique of repeated intention, the cells of the brain unify themselves to the will of the conscious mind. Over time the repeated intention becomes a command and a waypoint for focus and action. "I am rich" becomes an end point. As new cells replace old cells, "I am rich" becomes the dominant echo throughout the body. The cells will align themselves as a group to the command, producing desires and thoughts that will guide the person toward their goal. Individuals who invest in self-improvement through diet, basic securities, and development of the mind have the best chance of pursuing higher opportunities in life.

Excluding sinecures and legacy money, people get rich slowly, through decades of focused work, applied thought, patience, and faith in action. The individual grows to higher economic stations during the process; this requires health, vitality, and mental plasticity. Making the conscious choice to get rich is a commitment to health and personal development. As the individual improves their health, each new generation of cells produces a cumulative effect, which can eventually change the genetic regulating chemicals and cause a new pattern of gene expression. As the body's health improves, brain cells are bathed in nutrient-dense electromagnetic blood, improving focus and concentration. Over time the individual fundamentally changes in self-concept and appearance, which will cause a corresponding change to their environment.

CHAPTER 19:
MONEY AND WORK

The difference between poverty and wealth is subjective and relative. Values are personal, and therefore the definition of wealth is personal. Wealth is centered on money. The possession of money enables people to express themselves and to achieve the goals that satisfy their personal definitions of wealth.

In the book *The Power of Your Subconscious Mind*, Joseph Murphy states, "There is no virtue in poverty. It is a disease of the mind, and one should heal themselves of this mental conflict or malady at once."[212] Believing that poverty is an expression of mental illness reveals the shortcomings of simply increasing access to money for the poor. Conditions are established through behavior, and poverty is one of the potential cumulative effects of behavior.

Abject poverty was common in what is known as the Five Points in New York City during the mid-1800s. Efforts to revitalize these tenements were often obstructed by the tenants who lived in them. A wealthy philanthropist outfitted one of the tenement properties with stationary tubs, sanitary plumbing, wood closets, and all the latest improvements. The tenants used the wood closets for kindling, the pipes and faucets were ripped out and traded in for cash, the pipes were cut, and the tubs were used for various things other than bathing. Within three months the wealthy philanthropist removed what was left of his improvements. He joined a growing population that recognized that reforming or revitalizing a tenement requires an investment in the tenant as well. This example added credibility to a popular sentiment of the time: "Those who fight for the poor must fight the poor to do it."[213]

Mental illness or behavior that undermines a person's well-being can be found in all income classes. The austerity, sacrifices, and commitment to self-improvement necessary to get rich can languish as people reap the benefits of their hard work. Decadence, characterized by excess, moral decline, and self-centered indulgence, can be an expression of mental illness. When decadent behavior is practiced by a middle-class family, it will quickly lead to debt and poverty, while onlookers would be inclined to frame the behavior as an illness and offer sympathy. However, when a wealthy family adopts a lucullan lifestyle, it may be perceived as mammon, and invoke feelings of jealousy regardless of the similarities in behavior.

In action, the purpose of getting rich translates into helping as many people as possible. Bill Gates and Jeff Bezos became two of the wealthiest people on earth by creating Microsoft and Amazon, respectively. Both services have transformed society and positively affected the lives of people the world over. The viability and success of a company requires growth, adaptation, fiscal oversight, and innovation to stay relevant to consumers' needs and wants. An exceptional company will turn an original thought into a product or service that produces exponential growth, the way the internet has been used for e-commerce. Capitalism forces similar companies to compete for consumers, which demands innovation that leads to product or service improvement as well as price reduction. When the prices go down, more people can buy products or services, which leads to larger profits while positively affecting the lives of more people.

Save for local taxes, the money people spend often leaves the community they live in. In most cases, food, building materials, gas, automobiles, auto parts, clothing, and other routinely used goods and services are produced outside the community. A local company that grows their business can sell their products to other towns, states, and countries. The employees working for a successful business are paid with money from other parts of the world that they can spend locally. The influx of external capital will raise the vibrancy and desirability of a town or state.

The vibrancy of a community is also determined by its residents. When a person decides to get healthy, they also decide to get rich. A person's health determines their focus, energy, and self-expression. Likewise, money is a form of energy that is focused by the will of the owner to amplify their self-expression. Healthy people are prone to providing a higher quality of work, which makes them better employees and makes a company more successful, which in turn leads to more money. Society is held together by a shared commitment to providing reliable services and products to one another. When citizens start receiving shoddy, unreliable work from other community members, it threatens the cohesive strength of society. Moreover, it may inspire community members to act in kind, leading to further group destabilization. Conversely, providing reliable, trustworthy work can strengthen community ties and encourage others to raise their standard of work. Individuals who commit themselves to self-improvement and honest work will not only allow themselves to get rich; they will expect it. Raises and promotions increase an individual's income, but how they spend their money determines a person's wealth.

Getting rich is good for the environment. When people buy higher-quality goods and services, they tend to last longer. Having money allows people to keep up with maintenance that extends the life of their investments such as their home and car. Wealthy people can also help usher in new technology and innovation by being able to pay higher prices until a company or competitor can offer the same product at a lower cost. Wealthy people can invest in the changes they want to see in the world.

CHAPTER 20:
INVESTING IN THE STOCK MARKET

When a person sets their mind to becoming wealthy, the circumstance and lifestyle changes that follow are a fait accompli. The common practice to getting rich is saving 10 percent of one's income and investing it passively. Investing is a long-term practice; therefore, it is recommended that the individual save 10 percent of their income for six consecutive months before using earnings to invest. This way the individual will have money reserved for unexpected expenses without having to withdraw any money from long-term investments. In the United States, the average yearly raise and average yearly inflation rate is approximately 3.5 percent, which means that employees in static positions will experience a horizontal cost of living from year to year, barring unforeseen expenses. By saving 10 percent of their monthly take-home pay, an individual learns to live below their means and above the 3.5 percent inflation rate. Over time the restrictive spending lifestyle will develop peace of mind from a sense of financial security.

Eventually, the "pay yourself first" habit will become second nature without a noticeable difference in quality of life.

The most accessible and popular way to invest is through the stock market. The stock market is a place where individuals can buy and sell shares of publicly traded companies. Private companies can become public through an initial public offering (IPO) process.[214] Once a company is publicly listed, investors can purchase their shares. This allows the company to raise money and grow their business. In doing so, any investor who buys shares of the company can be considered part owner and a beneficiary of the success or failure the company experiences over time.

Brokerage accounts and individual retirement accounts (IRAs) are the main vehicles for investing in the stock market. A Roth IRA is money invested after taxes. A traditional IRA is money invested before taxes. As of 2022 the maximum amount an individual can contribute to either IRA is $6,000 a year ($7,000, fifty or older). Individuals who earn more than $144,000 a year or $204,000 when filing jointly are prohibited from adding to or opening a Roth IRA. There are no income restrictions for opening or adding to a traditional IRA or brokerage account.[215] The standard brokerage account is a taxable nonretirement account that provides individuals access to a broad range of investments, including the stock market. Any interest, dividends, or stocks sold at a profit are taxable. Stocks sold at a loss can also be taxed as negative income to reduce the account holder's gross annual salary (up to $3,000). Fidelity, Charles Schwab, E-Trade, Vanguard, Ally Invest, and Merrill are a few of the top-rated brokers where individuals can open either an IRA or brokerage account.[216]

Buying individual stocks or shares in a mutual fund and investing in the S&P 500 index are common options practiced by investors. The S&P 500 index was created in 1926. It originally included ninety companies; by 1957 the index consisted of five hundred companies.[217]

The five hundred companies in the S&P 500 index are the largest in the US economy by capital. The combined capitalization of these five hundred companies is roughly 80 percent of all publicly traded US companies. Therefore, investing in the S&P 500 index is investing in the US economy. From 1928 to 2006, the average annual return from the S&P 500 was 10.3 percent.[218] Jack Bogle created the first S&P 500 index fund in 1976, called the Vanguard Index Fund (now called the Vanguard 500 Index Fund (VOO)). The fund generated an average annual return of 12 percent from 1976 to 2006.[219] Over time an S&P 500 index fund will outperform mutual funds.[220]

S&P 500 Index

Decade	Average annual return (%)	Average annual dividend (%)
1980–1989	17.951	4.129
1990–1999	18.8	2.363
2000–2009	1.156	1.825
2010–2019	14.07	1.992

The average return on the S&P 500 from 1980 to 2019 was 12.99 percent, excluding inflation and expense ratio.

Equity mutual funds are collections of stocks curated by a fund manager. When an investor buys shares in an equity mutual fund, they are buying percentages of each stock in the fund's portfolio. Mutual funds present as a safe way to invest in the stock market because they offer the investor a diverse exposure to equities actively managed by an educated fund manager. There are several drawbacks to investing in mutual funds:

- Mutual funds have management and operating fees called an expense ratio. Expense ratios can cost the investor 3–3.5 percent a year in annual returns, regardless of the fund's performance.
- Many fund managers are responsible for investing billions of dollars, causing them to buy the biggest stocks so that they can make purchases in multimillion-dollar quantities.
- Investors tend to pour more money into mutual funds as the stock market rises, causing managers to buy overpriced, giant companies.
- Investors tend to sell their mutual fund shares when the stock market drops, forcing managers to sell stocks in the portfolio at low prices to pay their investors. (When investors buy into a mutual fund, they are subject to the behavior of other fund shareholders. If enough investors buy or sell shares of the mutual fund, the price will change.)
- Fund managers compulsively add stocks to their portfolio when it is included in the S&P 500 index.
- Managers are sometimes asked to create niche funds regardless of whether they like the stocks used to make those funds.
- The average fund does not pick stocks well enough to overcome the cost of researching and trading them.
- The higher the expense ratio, the lower the returns.
- When managers frequently change the fund's portfolio, it tends to earn less.

- Highly volatile funds stay volatile.
- Mutual funds with high past returns are unlikely to remain winners in the future.
- Fund managers limit the number of stocks in their portfolio, making the fund easy to monitor. This prevents managers from buying smaller, promising stocks.
- Federal law prohibits a fund from owning too much of one company's stock.
- High-performing "stock pickers" do not stay at firms for long because of high demand. Once the manager leaves the firm, their winning fund may become a loser.[221]

Investing and Trading

The typical mutual fund has an expense ratio of 3.5 percent. The Vanguard total stock market fund (S&P 500 index) has an expense ratio of 0.3 percent.[222] An expense ratio is the annual cost investors pay to have the fund managed. The graph below illustrates the power of compound return and the compound cost of investing $10,000 over forty years. The Vanguard stock market fund and a typical mutual fund are assumed to generate an average annual return of 10 percent. The annual return for an investor from each fund minus the expense ratio would be 10 percent − 0.3 percent = **9.7 percent** for the Vanguard total stock market fund and 10 percent − 3.5 percent = **6.5 percent** for the typical mutual fund.

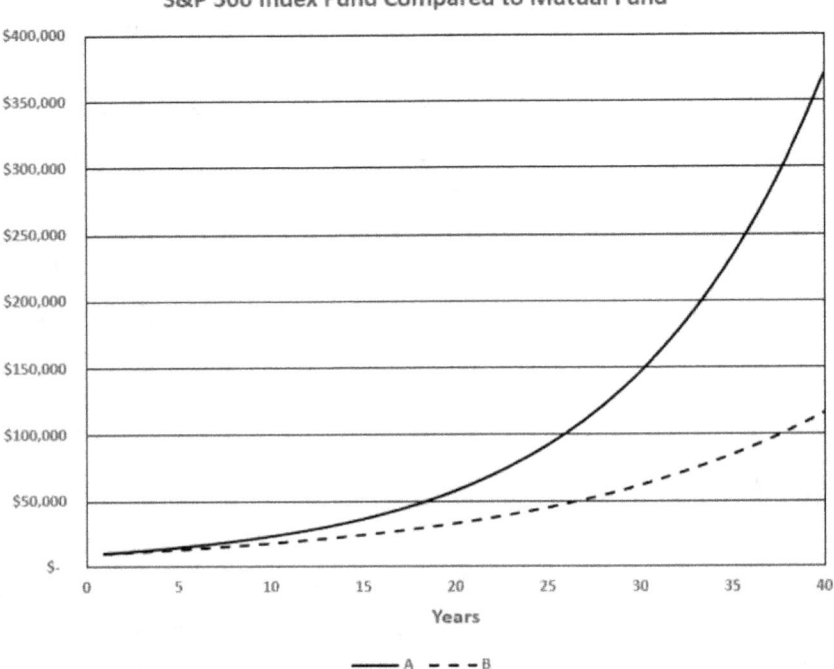

The Vanguard Index Fund (**A**) generated $369,878 from the initial $10,000 investment when left untouched for forty years. The typical mutual fund (**B**) returned $116,583. The compounding cost of inflation (3.5 percent) over 40 years translates to a spending power return of $104,437 from the Vanguard Index Fund and a mere $31,620 from investing in the typical mutual fund.

Once the habit of "paying yourself first" becomes ingrained, an investor will be able to add money regularly to their remunerative retirement account. The dollar cost averaging approach to investing means that the investor buys fewer shares when the market is up and more shares when the market is down, creating a satisfactory overall price.[223] The accretion from passively investing in the S&P 500 index through dollar cost averaging over several decades will generate peace of mind and a comfortable retirement.

The compound return from fixed annual contributions to an S&P 500 Index over 40 years.

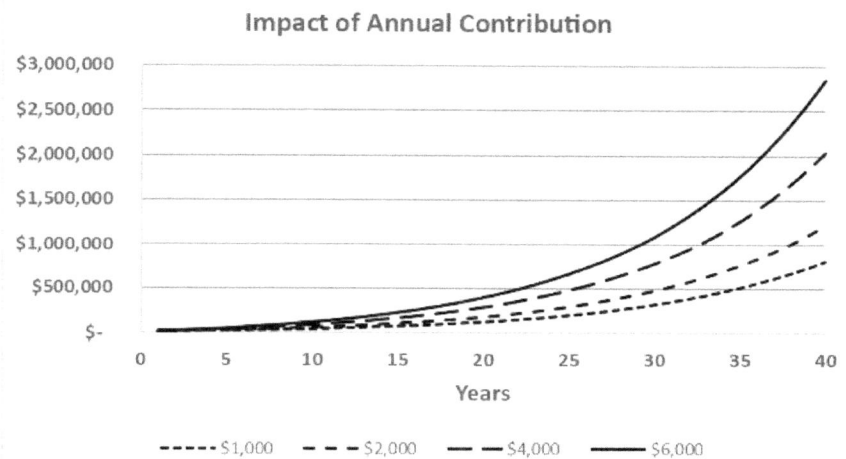

In most cases investors who buy individual stocks do so outside their ken. Moreover, fund managers routinely underperform relative to the S&P 500 index despite the stock market being their bailiwick. Nevertheless, many investors, through ignorance and compulsion, attempt to create their own portfolio of stocks in hopes of getting rich. Buying individual stocks is an active or enterprising form of investing that requires research and stability.

Investors are reactionary and prone to losing money in the stock market. People are pattern-seeking animals. If an event occurs two or three times in row, regions in the brain called the anterior cingulate and nucleus accumbens will automatically anticipate that it will happen again. When the event does happen again, the areas release dopamine, flooding the brain with a sense of euphoria.[224] Addictive drugs and sugar also increase dopamine levels in the nucleus accumbens.[225] The euphoria experienced from the spike in dopamine can lead to withdrawal as dopamine levels decrease. When the cycle is repeated enough times, the person or investor will develop a dependence on the trigger that caused the release in dopamine.

People who are addicted to dopamine are often characterized as compulsive with uncontrollable behavior. Investors who buy their own stocks are prone to stock market addiction. After watching a stock rise for several days in a row, they are likely to buy it, hoping it will go up further. When it does go up, they experience a high as dopamine levels rise. This automatic chemical reaction causes investors to buy overpriced stocks. Conversely, when an investor watches a stock they own drop in price for several consecutive days, it activates the amygdala, the area of the brain that processes fear and anxiety as well as the fight or flight response. The "pain" of watching their stock lose money is twice as intense as the pleasure of an equivalent gain in stock price. Many investors sell their position after the stock has dropped significantly (losing the investor money) to forgo any more pain from watching the price drop further. Moreover, the investor will often refuse to buy the stock again, despite the price being lower when they initially bought it, because of the experience. The emotional reactions hardwired in the brain produce natural tendencies to buy high and sell low. Active or enterprising investors who self-impose restrictions to buying and selling stocks will develop resistance to the compulsive behavior that leads to financial ruin.

Enterprising investors have better returns by trading less. The psychologist Paul Andreassen conducted an experiment in the late 1980s with MIT business students. He allowed the students to pick their own stocks, then separated them into two groups. One group was able to see the price of their stocks change with no other information. The other group was also able to watch the price fluctuations of their stocks but was given access to whatever financial information they wanted, which included financial news and TV, the *Wall Street Journal*, or even experts on the latest market trends. Many of the students became fixated on rumors and insider gossip, which led them to inaccurately predict financial trends as they tried to game the market. This caused the high-information group to engage in far more buying and selling than the group with less information. As a result, they earned only half as much as the low-information group.[226] Andreassen's experiment reveals that exposure to high amounts of information can lead to compulsive, shortsighted behavior, resulting in lower returns.

The experiment also focuses on the difference between stock market investing and speculative trading. Speculative traders buy and sell securities with a high probability of failure, seeking abnormally high returns over extremely short periods of time. Day trading is not considered gambling because traders are assumed to be making trades based on available information about the stock price, the company, and the market. However, speculative day trading creates a brain chemistry profile similar to that of drug users and gamblers, which suggests that those who make frequent trades are motivated to get intoxicated from trading rather than making money. Stock market investors build wealth slowly by taking on average or below-average risks and holding the position for a minimum of a year.

Investors buy company shares in the present as investments in an uncertain future. Successfully investing in the stock market means buying shares in a promising company at a fair or undervalued price and holding the position for several years. Investors use both known and unknown measurements to deduce the future of a company. Management, the anticipated demand for the product or service in the future, competition, supply and demand, inflation, interest rates, war, and commodity shortages are unknown future factors that can directly influence the success of a business. The company's size, financial conditions, acquisition history, earnings stability, dividend record, earnings growth, and price-to-earnings ratio are known factors established by a company's past performance.[227] Evaluating a company's previous success and the success of the current CEO is recommended before looking at any unknown future factors. Once an investor finds a promising company, they can use simple, established equations based on known measurements to determine whether the stock price is accurate for the current value and trajectory of the business.

Measuring a Stock: A Basic Overview

Revenue = average sale price × number of units sold. Revenue is money received from normal business activity each quarter. When evaluating a company's success and value, its revenue is considered the *top-line number*.

Price-to-earnings ratio (P/E) = the market-value price (stock price) ÷ the company's earnings per share (company's profit ÷ outstanding shares). When evaluating a company, the P/E is considered the *bottom-line number*. The higher the earnings per share, the lower the P/E. Fewer outstanding shares increases the earnings per share, lowering the P/E. A company with a P/E below fifteen is considered undervalued. A company with a P/E over eighteen is considered overvalued. The average P/E on the S&P is typically between thirteen and fifteen. A high P/E means that people are buying the stock. The trailing twelve-month (TTM) P/E is the company's known, measurable performance from the previous year. The forward P/E is a prediction of the company's performance for the year to come based on quarterly reports, public demand, and other variables. The forward P/E is a measurement of unknown factors.

Price-to-earnings-to-growth (PEG) = the market value price (stock price) ÷ earnings to growth. A stock's P/E ÷ the growth rate of its earnings over a specific time period. The PEG is used to determine the stock's current value and its expected earnings growth. A stock with a PEG of one or lower is considered undervalued.

Price-to-book ratio (P/B) = the market value price (stock price) ÷ book value (all assets − liabilities) ÷ shares outstanding. A stock with a P/B value under one is considered undervalued. Some analysts view a P/B under three to be undervalued. The P/B value can be industry specific.

Earnings per share (EPS) = company's net profit ÷ number of outstanding shares (common stock). The EPS indicates the company's profitability. A higher EPS will allow the company to increase its dividend. The EPS is relative to industries. Measuring a company's EPS over several years will help determine whether it is growing.

Debt-to-equity ratio (D/E) = the company's total liabilities ÷ shareholder equity. Shareholder equity is the company's net worth (assets − liabilities) that it can pay to its shareholders. The D/E ratio is used to evaluate a company's financial leverage by determining how much money the company is borrowing to finance its operations versus how much of its funds it wholly owns. A low D/E ratio means that the company is carrying less debt and is a safer investment in case it falls on hard times.

Free cash flow = the company's sales or revenue − sum of taxes and all operating costs. Free cash flow is the money the company has after its financial obligations are met.

Net income or net earnings = sales − the company's cost of providing their goods and services, including administrative costs, operating expenses, depreciation, interest, and taxes. Net income is the revenue made after expenses.

Diluted EPS = (the company's EPS − any preferred dividends) ÷ (outstanding shares + diluted shares [any additional shares the company has issued].

Net change in cash = net cash from operating activities + net cash used in investing activities + net cash used in financing activities. It is how much cash went into or out of the business in any time period.

Cost of revenue = total cost of manufacturing and delivering a product or service to consumers.

EBITDA = earnings before interest, taxes, depreciation, and amortization (paying off debts). EBITDA is a measure of a company's profits, excluding expenses.

Book value per share (BVPS) = equity available to common shareholders ÷ the number of outstanding shares. The BVPS determines the company's net assets on a per-share basis. If the company was liquidated, the BVPS is the money an investor would receive per share.

Dividend = a sum of money paid regularly (quarterly) by a company to its shareholders out of its profits or reserves. A dividend aristocrat is a company in the S&P 500 index that pays a dividend for at least twenty-five years while raising the dividend annually.[228]

The number of shares outstanding directly affects the relationship between the stock price and company performance.

Dividends, Earnings Growth, and Shares Outstanding

A company can directly recognize its shareholders through dividends, earnings growth, and the number of shares outstanding. A company can issue public and restricted shares. Restricted shares are reserved for private investors and company employees. The public shares or stock float are shares available for any investor to buy.[229]

Disparities in stock price and company performance result from the supply and demand that investors create when trading a stock. A company with a limited supply of shares available to trade will experience more dramatic fluctuations in price than a company with a high float from fewer investors buying and selling the stock. When a company executes a share buyback, it removes shares available to trade, lowering the float. Removing shares through a company buyback increases each remaining share's ownership percentage. When a company reduces the number of shares, it also positively affects the relationship between the stock price and company performance, attracting more investors.

Earnings growth is the change in net income over time, usually quarter to quarter or annually. Tracking net income allows the investor to determine whether the company is growing and whether it is managing its cost well in the process. Profitable companies have a positive EPS and P/E. Comparing a company's EPS over several quarters or years averages out irregularities in the business, allowing investors to accurately view the company's growth and money management. Investing in companies with a positive EPS will filter out zombies, companies that are unable to pay their debts and earn just enough to continue operating. They often have no excess capital to grow their business and have higher borrowing costs. A negative change in the economy may cause them to become insolvent and go out of business.[230]

Earnings growth and dividends are the two main sources for a stock's long-term return to investors.[231] As shareholder and part owner, investors are entitled to any profits realized by the company, which are paid out as dividends.[232] Dividends are usually paid to the investor quarterly as cash per share. An investor can reinvest the cash dividend by buying more shares or can use it for other investments. Dividends have buying power relative to the inflation rate and market conditions when they are issued. Aristocrat stocks are the stocks of companies that have raised their dividend annually for twenty-five years. An investor who buys and holds an aristocrat stock for twenty-five years will collect a yearly dividend while annually increasing their dollar per dividend yield rate, regardless of the stock price.

Coca-Cola is an aristocrat stock used below to illustrate the potential long-term return by holding a position continuously for twenty years. Disney, Pfizer, and Boeing were also chosen because of their size and name recognition. Biogen was selected because it did not pay a dividend between 2002 and 2022. Amazon and Apple were trading at $0.72 and $0.42 in January 2002, making them relatively obscure and unattractive to risk-averse long-term investors at that time. The Vanguard Total Market Index Fund outperformed the stocks listed above over a twenty-year period.

The Cumulative Twenty-Year Return for PFE, KO, BA, BIIB, DIS, and VTI

Disney stock price return: January 2002–January 2022

Buy price	Sell price	Return	Percent return
$21.00	$137.38	$116.38	554.2 percent

Disney dividend yield per dollar: January 2002–January 2022

Buy price = $21.00	Initial annual dividend = $0.21	Final annual dividend = $0
	Initial dividend yield on dollar invested = 1 percent	Final dividend yield on dollar invested = 0 percent

Disney dividend return: January 2002–January 2022

Disney paid a variable dividend over the twenty-year period. In 2020 the company suspended its dividend. The cumulative dividend return paid to the investor from January 2002 to January 2022 was $13.70.

Total return to investor: $116.38 + $13.70 = $130.08 or 619.42 percent.

Biogen stock price return: January 2002–January 2022

Buy price	Sell price	Return	Percent return
$60.733	$241.52	$180.787	297.67506 percent

Biogen does not offer a dividend.

Total return to investor: $180.787 or 297.675 percent.

Boeing stock price return: January 2002–January 2022

Buy price	Sell price	Return	Percent return
$30.00	$205.44	$175.44	584.8 percent

Boeing dividend yield per dollar: January 2002–January 2022

Buy price = $30.00	Initial annual dividend = $0.68	Final annual dividend = $0
	Initial dividend yield on dollar invested = 2.26 percent	Final dividend yield on dollar invested = 0 percent

Boeing dividend return: January 2002–January 2022.

Boeing paid a variable dividend over the twenty-year period. In 2020 the company suspended its dividend. The cumulative dividend return paid to the investor from January 2002 to January 2022 was $51.54.

Total return to investor: $175.44 + $51.54 = $226.98 or 756.6 percent.

Coca-Cola stock price return: January 2002–January 2022

Buy price	Sell price	Return	Percent return
$23.22	$60.33 x 2= 120.66*	$97.44	419.63 percent

*In 2012 the stock split two for one.

Coca-Cola dividend yield per dollar: January 2002–January 2022

Buy price = $23.22	Initial annual dividend = $0.8	Final annual dividend = $1.68 x 2 =3.36*
	Initial dividend yield on dollar invested = 3.445 percent	Final dividend yield on dollar invested = 14.47 percent*

*In 2012 the stock split two for one.

Coca-Cola dividend return: January 2002–January 2022

Coca-Cola is an aristocrat stock. Coca-Cola offered a continuous dividend for the entire twenty years. The company also raised the dividend annually. The cumulative return to the investor from January 2002 to January 2022 was $40.97.

Total return to investor: $97.44 + $40.97 = $138.41 or 596.08 percent.

Pfizer stock price return: January 2002–January 2022

Buy price	Sell price	Return	Percent return
$38.46	$55.72	$17.26	44.87 percent

Pfizer dividend yield per dollar: January 2002–January 2022

Buy price = $38.46	Initial annual dividend = $0.52	Final annual dividend = $1.56
	Initial dividend yield on dollar invested = 1.35 percent	Final dividend yield on dollar invested 4.056 percent

Pfizer dividend return: January 2002–January 2022

Pfizer is not an aristocrat stock but has paid a continuous dividend since 2002. The cumulative return to the investor from January 2002 to January 2022 was $22.427.

Total return to investor: $17.26 + $22.427 = $39.687 or 103.19 percent.

VTI (Vanguard Total Stock Market Index Fund) stock price return: January 2002–January 2022

Buy price	Sell price	Return	Percent return
$52.36	235.02 x 2 = $470.04*	$417.68	797.708 percent

*VTI split two for one in 2008.

VTI dividend yield per dollar: January 2002–January 2022

Buy price = $52.36	Initial annual dividend = $1.252	Final annual dividend = $2.9303 x 2 = 5.8606*
	Initial dividend yield on dollar invested = 2.391 percent	Final dividend yield on dollar invested = 11.19 percent*

*VTI split two for one in 2008.

VTI dividend return: January 2002–January 2022.
VTI has paid a continuous variable dividend since 2002. The cumulative return to the investor from January 2002 to January 2022 was $66.681.

Total return to investor: $417.68 + $66.681= $484.361 or 925.05 percent.

The Importance of Researching Stocks

An active, enterprising investor must do research to buy successful individual stocks. The internet is a heuristic tool for investors replete with salespeople, hucksters, bunkum, and econobabble. Most financial news and online investment magazines are designed to increase the frequency of stock trading, which will lead to lower returns over time. Like printed market brochures, these websites and TV stations are platforms to sell products (in this case, stocks) to the consumer regardless of a company's intrinsic potential or current stock price. Investors that exclusively resign themselves to these "research" vehicles are better off investing in the S&P 500 index. Looking a gift horse in the mouth prevents consumers from buying a pig in a poke. By directly researching companies, their competitors, current and future economic demand, and stock price valuations, investors will be able to accurately and intelligently buy promising stocks at a fair value.

Here is a basic investing strategy:
- History of paying a dividend with a current yield of 5 percent or higher.
- P/E below ten.
- A positive EPS for a minimum of three years.
- Hold for a fixed amount of time or strategically sell.

Over time, the aggregate gains earned by the shareholder must by necessity match the business gains of the company.[233] Knowing this, long-term investors often ignore the irrational, speculative exuberance that can cause dramatic price volatility for individual stocks. However, investors can strategically sell a portion of their position when a stock they own experiences a price bubble. Strategic selling is premeditated and therefore is not part of the emotional, addictive behavior that comes with trading equities.

MICHAEL SIMMONS

Here is an example of a strategic selling outcome over one year:

An investor spends $5,000 buying one hundred shares of company X at $50 a share with a 5 percent dividend. The dividend is paid quarterly: $50 ÷ 100 = $0.5 × 5 = $2.5 ÷ 4 = $0.625 per share per quarter. The investor is set up to automatically sell 20 percent (twenty shares) of the position when the stock price rises 20 percent ($60) and leave 80 percent (eighty shares) as a long-term position.

Q1	Q2	Q3	Strategic sell*	Q4	Total
100 shares × $0.625 = $62.5	100 shares × $0.625 = $62.5	100 shares × $0.625 = $62.5	Do not sell any stock	100 shares × $0.625 = $62.5	$250 with 100 shares
100 shares × $0.625 = $62.5	100 shares × $0.625 = $62.5	100 shares × $0.625 = $62.5	Sell 20 shares at $60 per share = $1,200*	80 shares × $0.625 = $50	$1,437.5 with 80 shares*

*The total return on the year depends on what quarter the stock price goes up 20 percent.

A strategic selling approach like the one outlined above will give the investor additional liquidity during a contracted time horizon. The realized return and any other money contributed that year will allow the investor to buy another security earlier in their investing career, abbreviating the time needed to create their own portfolio of promising stocks. As a general rule, the longer someone is able to keep money in the market, the higher their return. The earlier people start investing, the more likely they are to achieve a comfortable retirement.

Endnotes

1 Thomas Troward, *The Edinburgh Lectures on Mental Science* (Radford, VA: Wilder Publications, 2008), 11.

2 C. L. Ralph, "The Pineal Gland and Geographical Distribution of Animals," *International Journal of Biometeorology* 19 (December 1975): 289–303.

3 Berel Lang, *Race and Racism in Theory and Practice* (London: Rowman & Littlefield, 2000), 10–11.

4 Donald Voet and Judith G. Voet, *Biochemistry*, 4th ed. (Hoboken, NJ: John Wiley & Sons, 2011).

5 Andrzej Slominski and Arnold E Postlethwaite. "Skin under the Sun: When Melanin Pigment Meets Vitamin D," *Endocrinology* 156, no. 1 (2015): 1–4, doi:10.1210/en.2014-1918.

6 Wallace D. Wattles, *The Science of Getting Rich, the Science of Being Well, the Science of Being Great, and the Law of Opulence* (Limitless Press, 2010), 84.

7 Robert O. Becker and Gary Selden, *The Body Electric: Electromagnetism and the Foundation of Life* (New York: William Morrow, 1985), 121.

8 Farzaneh A. Sorond et al., "Cerebral Blood Flow Regulation during Cognitive Tasks: Effects of Healthy Aging," *Cortex* 44, no. 2 (2008): 179–184, https://doi.org/10.1016/j.cortex.2006.01.003.

9 W. M. Snow et al., "Chronic Dietary Creatine Enhances Hippocampal-Dependent Spatial Memory, Bioenergetics, and Levels of Plasticity-Related Proteins Associated with NF-⊠B," *Learning and Memory* 25, no. 2 (January 2018): 54–66, doi: 10.1101/lm.046284.117.

10 A. I. Abd Hamid et al., "Brain Activation during Addition and Subtraction Tasks In-Noise and In-Quiet," *The Malaysian Journal of Medical Sciences* 18, no. 2 (April 2011): 3–15.

11 Wattles, *The Science of Getting Rich*, 84.

12 L. O. Lee et al., "Optimism Is Associated with Exceptional Longevity in 2 Epidemiologic Cohorts of Men and Women," *Proceedings of the National Academy of Sciences of the USA* 116, no. 37 (September 2019): 18357–18362, doi: 10.1073/pnas.1900712116.

13 M. T. Pänkäläinen, T. V. Kerola, and J. J. Hintikka, "Pessimism and the Risk for Coronary Heart Disease among Middle-Aged and Older Finnish Men and Women: A Ten-Year Follow-Up Study," *BMC Cardiovascular Disorders* 15 (October 2015): 113, doi: 10.1186/s12872-015-0097-y.

14 R. Chetty et al., "The Association between Income and Life Expectancy in the United States, 2001–2014," *The Journal of the American Medical Association*, 315, no. 16 (April 2016):1750–1766, doi: 10.1001/jama.2016.4226; Erratum, *The Journal of the American Medical Association*, 317, no. 1 (January 2017): 90.

15 Wattles, *The Science of Getting Rich*, 8.

16 William Walker Atkinson, *Thought Force in Business and Everyday Life* (McAllister Editions, 2015), 15–19.

17 Franz Bardon, *Initiation into Hermetics*, ed. Ken Johnson, trans. Gerhard Hanswille and Franca Gallo (Holladay, UT: Merkur Publishing, 1999), 82–83.

18 Patañjali, *How to Know God: The Yoga Aphorisms of Patanjali*, trans. Swami Prabhavananda and Christopher Isherwood (London: Allen & Unwin, 1953), 59–60.

19 Swami Sivananda, *Thought Power*, 6th ed. (Uttar Pradesh, India: Divine Life Society, 1980), 31.

20 Becker and Selden, *The Body Electric*, 277–278.

21 Z. L. Hutchison et al., "Anthropogenic Electromagnetic Fields (EMF) Influence the Behaviour of Bottom-Dwelling Marine Species," *Scientific Reports* 10, no. 1 (March 2020): 4219, doi: 10.1038/s41598-020-60793-x.

22 Eric Hand, "The Body's Hidden Compass—What Is It, and How Does It Work?," *Science*, June 23, 2016, doi: 10.1126/science.aaf5804.

23 R. R. Baker, J. G. Mather, and J. H. Kennaugh, "Magnetic Bones in Human Sinuses," *Nature* 301, no. 5895 (January 1983): 79–80, doi: 10.1038/301096b0.

24 T. J. Nakamura et al., "Circadian and Photic Regulation of Cryptochrome mRNAs in the Rat Pineal Gland," *Neuroscience Research* 41, no. 1 (September 2001): 25–32, doi: 10.1016/s0168-0102(01)00255-3.

25 Douglas C. Giancoli, *Physics: Principles with Applications*, 6th ed. (Boston: Pearson, 2005), 615.

26 Jerry Tennant, *Healing Is Voltage: The Handbook*, 3rd ed. (North Charleston, SC: CreateSpace, 2013), 92.

27 "4.5: The Cytoskeleton," Biology LibreTexts, April 9, 2022, https://bio.libretexts.org/Bookshelves/Introductory_and_General_Biology/General_Biology_1e_(OpenStax)/2%3A_The_Cell/04%3A_Cell_Structure/4.5%3A_The_Cytoskeleton.

28 Becker and Selden, *The Body Electric*, 276.

29 Samael Aun Weor, *The Perfect Matrimony*, 7th ed. (Old Saybrook, CT: Glorian Publishing, 2012), 67.

30 Becker and Selden, *The Body Electric*, 86, 95.

31 Tennant, *Healing Is Voltage*, 98–100.

32 Ibid., 101.

33 Becker and Selden, *The Body Electric*, 122.

34 Neil A. Campbell et al., *Biology: Concepts and Connections*, 4th ed. (New York: Pearson Education, 2003), 477.

35 Tennant, *Healing Is Voltage*, 92.

36 Voet and Voet, *Biochemistry*, 381, 511–512, 760, 764; Campbell et al., *Biology*, 436; Nicola Reavley, *The New Encyclopedia of Vitamins, Minerals, Supplements and Herbs* (Melbourne: Bookman, 1998), 220.

37 William A. McGarey, *Edgar Cayce on Healing Foods for Body, Mind, and Spirit* (Virginia Beach, VA: A.R.E. Press, 2002), 55–59.

38 Peter Tompkins and Christopher Bird, *The Secret Life of Plants* (New York: Harper & Row, 1973), 7.

39 Franz Bardon, *Initiation*, 31.

40 Sivananda, *Thought Power*, 11.

41 Gururattan Kaur Khalsa and Ann Marie Maxwell, eds., *Transitions to a Heart Centered World: Through the Kundalini Yoga and Meditations of Yogi Bhajan* (Coronado, CA: Yoga Technology Press, 1988), 23.

42 Swami Niranjanananda Saraswati, *Prana and Pranayama* (New Delhi, India: Yoga Publications Trust, 2009), 223–246.

43 Swami Vivekananda, *Living at the Source: Yoga Teachings of Vivekananda*, ed. Ann Myren and Dorothy Madison (Boston: Shambhala, 1993), 81.

44 Bardon, *Initiation*, 38–39.

45 Roger R. Hock, *Forty Studies That Changed Psychology* (Upper Saddle River, NJ: Prentice Hall, 2021), 51–53.

46 Tom Corbett and Lady Stearn Robinson, *Dreamer's Dictionary* (New York: Grand Central Publishing, 1974), 149, 179, 250, 256, 282, 326.

47 Habib Yaribeygi et al., "The Impact of Stress on Body Function: A Review," *EXCLI Journal* 16 (July 2017): 1057–1072, doi:10.17179/excli2017-480.

48 David F. Santana et al., "Maternal Protein Restriction in Two Successive Generations Impairs Mitochondrial Electron Coupling in the Progeny's

Brainstem of Wistar Rats from Both Sexes," *Frontiers in Neuroscience* 13, no. 203 (March 2019), doi:10.3389/fnins.2019.00203.

49   L. E. Caulfield et al., "Stunting, Wasting, and Micronutrient Deficiency Disorders," in *Disease Control Priorities in Developing Countries*, 2nd ed., ed. D. T. Jamison et al. (Washington, DC: International Bank for Reconstruction and Development/World Bank, 2006), chap. 28, https://www.ncbi.nlm.nih.gov/books/NBK11761/.

50   Patrick Drake and Jennifer Tolbert, "Key Facts about the Uninsured Population," Kaiser Family Foundation, December 19, 2022, https://www.kff.org/uninsured/issue-brief/key-facts-about-the-uninsured-population/.

51   Reavley, *The New Encyclopedia*, 646, 648.

52   Benjamin Franklin Museum.

53   Kreutler, *Nutrition in Perspective*, 245, 247.

54   William Walsh, *Nutrient Power: Heal Your Biochemistry and Heal Your Brain* (New York: Skyhorse Publishing, 2014), 37–43, 121–125, 191.

55   P. M. B. Walker, *Chambers Dictionary of Science and Technology* (Edinburgh: Chambers, 1999), 358.

56   Patricia A. Kreutler and Dorice M. Czajka-Narins, *Nutrition in Perspective* (Englewood Cliffs, NJ: Prentice-Hall, 1980), 580, 581.

57   "Wernicke-Korsakoff Syndrome," National Institute of Neurological Disorders and Stroke, US Department of Health and Human Services, January 31, 2023, https://www.ninds.nih.gov/health-information/disorders/wernicke-korsakoff-syndrome#:~:text=Korsakoff%20syndrome%20.

58   William H. Philpott and Dwight K. Kalita, *Brain Allergies*, 2nd ed. (Los Angeles: Keats Publishing, 1980), 106–109.

59   "The Connection between Homelessness and Addiction," Michael's House, https://www.michaelshouse.com/drug-abuse/study-homelessness-addiction/.

60   L. B. Wilson et al., "Do Dual Purchasers Behave Differently? An Analysis of Purchasing Data for Households That Buy Both Alcohol and Tobacco in the United Kingdom," *Addiction* 116 (2021): 2538–2547, https://doi.org/10.1111/add.15430.

61   B. Nyakutsikwa, J. Britton, and T. Langley, "The Effect of Tobacco and Alcohol Consumption on Poverty in the United Kingdom," *Addiction* 116 (2021): 150–158, https://doi.org/10.1111/add.15096.

62 "Nutrition Gap between Rich and Poor Is Growing, but Don't Blame Food Deserts, Researchers Say," University of Chicago Booth School of Business, February 13, 2018, https://www.chicagobooth.edu/media-relations-and-communications/press-releases/nutrition-gap-between-rich-and-poor-is-growing-but-dont-blame-food-deserts.

63 Marina Nikolić et al., "Identifying Critical Nutrient Intake in Groups at Risk of Poverty in Europe: The CHANCE Project Approach," *Nutrients* 6, no. 4 (April 2014): 1374–1393, doi:10.3390/nu6041374

64 Ibid.

65 Dylan Walsh, "The Roots of Nutritional Inequality," Stanford Graduate School of Business, January 26, 2018, https://www.gsb.stanford.edu/insights/roots-nutritional-inequality.

66 "Eating Healthy vs. Unhealthy Diet Costs about $1.50 More per Day," Harvard T. H. Chan School of Public Health, December 5, 2013, https://www.hsph.harvard.edu/news/press-releases/healthy-vs-unhealthy-diet-costs-1-50-more/.

67 Alana Rhone and Michele Ver Ploeg, "US Shoppers' Access to Multiple Food Stores Varies by Region," USDA Economic Research Service, June 3, 2019, https://www.ers.usda.gov/amber-waves/2019/june/us-shoppers-access-to-multiple-food-stores-varies-by-region/.

68 Elizabeth Kneebone, "The Changing Geography of US Poverty," Brookings, February 15, 2017, https://www.brookings.edu/testimonies/the-changing-geography-of-us-poverty/.

69 Hunt Allcott et al., "Food Deserts and the Causes of Nutritional Inequality," National Bureau of Economic Research, December 18, 2017, https://www.nber.org/papers/w24094.

70 Kathleen Park Talaro, *Foundations in Microbiology*, 5th ed. (New York: McGraw-Hill, 2005), 384.

71 Michael Simmons, "Gut (Pt6): Comprehensive look at GUT BACTERIA, PROBIOTICS, and CANDIDA," YouTube, April 21, 2020,

72 Ibid.

73 Michael Simmons, "Mitochondria Pt2: Anatomy, Bacterial Ancestry, Antibiotics, Iron (Fe)/Sulfur (S), Poisons," YouTube, March 27, 2019, https://www.youtube.com/watch?v=-dkZBCar1JA.

74 "Great Oxidation Event," Wikipedia, accessed January 28, 2023, https://en.wikipedia.org/wiki/Great_Oxidation_Event.

75 Tennant, *Healing Is Voltage*, 92, 289.

76 Simmons, "Mitochondria Pt2."

77 Campbell et al., *Biology*, 104–105.

78 Michael Simmons, "MOLD, YEAST, FUNGI: Cancer (Warburg), Antibiotics, Mitochondria," YouTube, September 28, 2020, https://www.youtube.com/watch?v=LSlAO1H5mFg&t=384s.

79 Michael Simmons, "Mitochondria Pt 1—Converting Sugar to Energy, the Vitamins and Minerals Required," YouTube, March 18, 2019, https://www.youtube.com/watch?v=UQFYuJnduWM.

80 Michael Simmons, "[Pt3] Anemia: How Exercise Causes Anemia, Mitochondria, Glucose, ATP, Fe, Red Blood Cells," YouTube, December 22, 2019, https://www.youtube.com/watch?v=KuFJ98zSg8Q.

81 Simmons, "Gut (Pt6)."

82 Giulia Enders, *Gut: The Inside Story of Our Body's Most Underrated Organ*, trans. Jill Enders and David Shaw (Vancouver: Greystone Books, 2015), 128.

83 Ibid., 134, 136.

84 Michael Simmons, "GUT (Pt4): Brain, Vagus Nerve, Depression, Probiotics, Anxiety, ParaSympathetic Nervous System," YouTube, March 27, 2020, https://www.youtube.com/watch?v=ss76g4MyQ3k&t=275s.

85 Enders, *Gut*, 128

86 Dan Brennan, ed., "Dysbiosis: Gut Imbalance, IBD, and More," WebMD, December 6, 2022, https://www.webmd.com/digestive-disorders/what-is-dysbiosis.

87 Tim Jewell, "What Causes Dysbiosis and How Is It Treated?," ed. Saurabh Sethi, Healthline, February 1, 2019, https://www.healthline.com/health/digestive-health/dysbiosis.

88 Simmons, "Gut (Pt6)."

89 Talaro, *Foundations in Microbiology*, 142, 144.

90 Roberto Pérez-Torrado and Amparo Querol, "Opportunistic Strains of *Saccharomyces cerevisiae*: A Potential Risk Sold in Food Products," *Frontiers in Microbiology* 6, no. 1522 (January 2016), doi:10.3389/fmicb.2015.01522.

91 Jorge Caldeira et al., "Saccharomycin, a Biocide from *S. cerevisiae* That Kill-Off Other Yeasts," *Annals of Medicine*, 51, no. S1 (2019): 94–95, DOI: 10.1080/07853890.2018.1562694.

92 "Beta-Alanine," Health Matters, 2019, https://healthmatters.io/understand-blood-test-results/beta-alanine-2.

93 Chih-Yung Chiu et al., "Gut Microbial-Derived Butyrate Is Inversely Associated with IgE Responses to Allergens in Childhood Asthma," *Pediatric Allergy and Immunology* 30, no. 7 (2019): 689–697, doi:10.1111/pai.13096.

94 "Beta-Alanine."

95 Kalina Duszka, "Taurine, Bile Acids, and Microbiota," Scholarly Community Encyclopedia, August 16, 2022, https://encyclopedia.pub/entry/history/show/63749.

96 Ibid.

97 Harris Ripps and Wen Shen, "Review: Taurine: A 'Very Essential' Amino Acid," *Molecular Vision* 18 (2012): 2673–2686.

98 Mark F. McCarty, "A Taurine-Supplemented Vegan Diet May Blunt the Contribution of Neutrophil Activation to Acute Coronary Events," *Medical Hypotheses* 63, no. 3 (2004): 419–425, doi:10.1016/j.mehy.2004.03.040.

99 Christine Ruggeri, "Sam-E: Benefits, Uses, Risks, Side Effects, Dosage and More," Dr. Axe, November 17, 2018, https://draxe.com/nutrition/sam-e/.

100 Ibid.

101 Joseph Pizzorno, "Glutathione!," *Integrative Medicine* 13, no. 1 (2014): 8–12.

102 Michael Simmons, "(2) MOLD, YEAST, FUNGI: Yeast vs Mold, Benefits and Diseases," YouTube, August 25, 2020, https://www.youtube.com/watch?v=C_0A68VAeek.

103 Tennant, *Healing Is Voltage*, 535; Elizabeth Lipski, *Digestive Wellness* (Lincolnwood, IL: Keats Publishing, 2000), 85.

104 Talaro, *Foundations in Microbiology*, 337–342.

105 "Facts + Statistics: Pet Ownership and Insurance," Insurance Information Institute, 2023, https://www.iii.org/fact-statistic/facts-statistics-pet-ownership-and-insurance.

106 "CDC—Toxoplasmosis," Centers for Disease Control and Prevention, August 29, 2018, https://www.cdc.gov/parasites/toxoplasmosis/index.html#:~:text=Toxoplasmosis%20is%20considered%20to%20be,the%20parasite%20from%20causing%20illness.

107 Enders, *Gut*, 212, 214, 215.

108 Wai Kit Chew et al., "Significant Reduction of Brain Cysts Caused by *Toxoplasma gondii* after Treatment with Spiramycin Coadministered with Metronidazole in a Mouse Model of Chronic Toxoplasmosis," *Antimicrobial*

	Agents and Chemotherapy 56, no. 4 (2012): 1762–1768. doi:10.1128/AAC.05183-11.
109	"CDC—Toxoplasmosis."
110	*Global Pet Sitting Market Size, Share & Trends Report, 2030*, Grand View Research, https://www.grandviewresearch.com/industry-analysis/pet-sitting-market.
111	I. Ghasemzadeh and S. H. Namazi, "Review of Bacterial and Viral Zoonotic Infections Transmitted by Dogs," in special issue, *Journal of Medicine and Life* 8, no. 4 (2015): 1–5.
112	Tennant, *Healing Is Voltage*, 92, 518–519.
113	Nicholas Zill, "The Paradox of Adoption," Institute for Family Studies, October 7, 2015, https://ifstudies.org/blog/the-paradox-of-adoption/.
114	T. A. Judge, C. Hurst, and L. S. Simon, "Does It Pay to Be Smart, Attractive, or Confident (or All Three)? Relationships among General Mental Ability, Physical Attractiveness, Core Self-Evaluations, and Income," *Journal of Applied Psychology* 94, no. 3 (2009): 742–755, https://doi.org/10.1037/a0015497.
115	"Stanford Prison Experiment," Wikipedia, accessed February 3, 2023, https://en.wikipedia.org/wiki/Stanford_prison_experiment.
116	*Webster's New Collegiate Dictionary*, 8[th, s.v. "jealousy"]
117	Robert B. Cialdini, *Pre-suasion: A Revolutionary Way to Influence and Persuade* (New York: Simon & Schuster, 2016), 158.
118	Cialdini, *Pre-suasion*, 122.
119	T. Wu et al., "The Capacity of Cognitive Control Estimated from a Perceptual Decision Making Task," *Scientific Reports* 6 (2016): 34025, https://doi.org/10.1038/srep34025.
120	Emily Kwong, "Understanding Unconscious Bias," NPR, July 15, 2020, https://www.npr.org/2020/07/14/891140598/understanding-unconscious-bias.
121	"The Psychology of Attraction: Why Do We Fancy Certain People?," BBC Bitesize, October 4, 2019, https://www.bbc.co.uk/bitesize/articles/zm9ry9q.
122	Joe Navarro and Marvin Karlins, *What Every Body Is Saying: An Ex-FBI Agent's Guide to Speed-Reading People* (New York: Harper Collins, 2008), 23–34.
123	Navarro and Karlins, *What Every Body Is Saying*, 39–43.

124 Chad Boutin, "Snap Judgments Decide a Face's Character, Psychologist Finds," Princeton University, August 22, 2006, https://www.princeton.edu/news/2006/08/22/snap-judgments-decide-faces-character-psychologist-finds.

125 Andreas Moritz, *Liver and Gallbladder Miracle Cleanse: An All-Natural, At-Home Flush to Purify and Rejuvenate Your Body* (Berkeley, CA: Ulysses Press, 2007), 65–75.

126 Judge, Hurst, and Simon, "Does It Pay."

127 Judge, Hurst, and Simon, "Does It Pay."

128 Anne C. Krendl et al., "The Good, the Bad, and the Ugly: An fMRI Investigation of the Functional Anatomic Correlates of Stigma," *Social Neuroscience* 1, no. 1 (2006), 5–15, https://krendlab.sitehost.iu.edu/upload/Krendl_et.al_2006.pdf.

129 Takashi Tsukiura et al., "Insular and Hippocampal Contributions."

130 Q. Luo et al., "The Neural Correlates of Integrated Aesthetics between Moral and Facial Beauty," *Scientific Reports* 9 (2019): 1980, https://doi.org/10.1038/s41598-019-38553-3.

131 Kim Parker, "Americans See Different Expectations for Men and Women," Pew Research Center's Social and Demographic Trends Project, Pew Research Center, August 6, 2020, https://www.pewresearch.org/social-trends/2017/12/05/americans-see-different-expectations-for-men-and-women/.

132 Reuters Staff, "Feeling Pretty? Hormones May Lead to More...," Reuters, January 14, 2009, https://www.reuters.com/article/us-estrogen-affairs/feeling-pretty-hormones-may-lead-to-more-idUSTRE50D03O20090114.

133 "Gynoid Fat Distribution," Wikipedia, January 30, 2023, https://en.wikipedia.org/wiki/Gynoid_fat_distribution#cite_note-7.

134 C. Soler et al., "Facial Attractiveness in Men Provides Clues to Semen Quality," *Evolution and Human Behavior* 24, no. 3 (2003): 199–207, https://doi.org/10.1016/S1090-5138(03)00013-8.

135 J. Verhaeghe et al., "Pheromones and Their Effect on Women's Mood and Sexuality," *Facts, Views and Vision* 5, no. 3 (2013): 189–195.

136 D. Gil et al., "Male Attractiveness and Differential Testosterone Investment in Zebra Finch Eggs," *Science* 286, no. 5437 (1999): 126–128, doi:10.1126/science.286.5437.126.

137 Randy Thornhill et al., "Major Histocompatibility Complex Genes, Symmetry, and Body Scent Attractiveness in Men and Women," *Behavioral*

138   *Ecology* 14, no. 5 (September 2003): 668–678, https://doi.org/10.1093/beheco/arg043.

138   Navneet Magon and Sanjay Kalra, "The Orgasmic History of Oxytocin: Love, Lust, and Labor," *Indian Journal of Endocrinology and Metabolism* 15, S3 (2011): S156–S161, doi:10.4103/2230-8210.84851.

139   Mac E. Hadley, *Endocrinology*, 5th ed. (Upper Saddle River, NJ: Prentice Hall, 2000), 146.

140   S. Ruggles, "The Rise of Divorce and Separation in the United States, 1880–1990," *Demography* 34, no. 4 (1997): 455–579, doi:10.2307/3038300.

141   "World War II: 1939–1945," Striking Women, Arts and Humanities Research Council, https://www.striking-women.org/module/women-and-work/world-war-ii-1939-1945.

142   "The First Measured Century: Book: Section 4.6," PBS, https://www.pbs.org/fmc/book/4family6.htm.

143   Shelby B. Scott et al., "Reasons for Divorce and Recollections of Premarital Intervention: Implications for Improving Relationship Education," *Couple and Family Psychology* 2, no. 2 (2013): 131–145, doi:10.1037/a0032025.

144   Jane Anderson, "The Impact of Family Structure on the Health of Children: Effects of Divorce," *Linacre Quarterly* 81, no. 4 (2014): 378–387, doi:10.1179/0024363914Z.00000000087.

145   Ibid.

146   F. H. Jónsson et al., "Parental Divorce: Long-Term Effects on Mental Health, Family Relations and Adult Sexual Behavior," *Scandinavian Journal of Psychology* 41, no. 2 (2000): 101–105, doi:10.1111/1467-9450.00177.

147   Bruce J. Ellis et al., "Does Father Absence Place Daughters at Special Risk for Early Sexual Activity and Teenage Pregnancy?," *Child Development* 74, no. 3 (2003): 801–821, doi:10.1111/1467-8624.00569.

148   J. Teachman, "Premarital Sex, Premarital Cohabitation, and the Risk of Subsequent Marital Dissolution among Women," *Journal of Marriage and Family* 65 (2003): 444–455, https://doi.org/10.1111/j.1741-3737.2003.00444.x.

149   Marnia Robinson, *Cupid's Poisoned Arrow: From Habit to Harmony in Sexual Relationships* (Berkeley, CA: North Atlantic Books, 2009), 23.

150   Ibid., 51.

151   Chloé Bouarab et al., "VTA GABA Neurons at the Interface of Stress and Reward," *Frontiers in Neural Circuits* 13, no. 78 (December 2019), doi:10.3389/fncir.2019.00078.

152   Robinson, *Cupid's Poisoned Arrow*, 118.

153   Ibid., 109.

154   Ibid., 119–120.

155   Daniel J. Tobiansky et al., "Androgen Regulation of the Mesocorticolimbic System and Executive Function," *Frontiers in Endocrinology* 9 279. 5 Jun. 2018, doi:10.3389/fendo.2018.00279

156   Hadley, *Endocrinology*.

157   Kay-Tee Khaw et al., "Endogenous Testosterone and Mortality Due to All Causes, Cardiovascular Disease, and Cancer in Men: European Prospective Investigation into Cancer in Norfolk (EPIC-Norfolk) Prospective Population Study," *Circulation* 116, no. 23 (2007): 2694–2701, doi:10.1161/CIRCULATIONAHA.107.719005.

158   Anne Harding, "Men's Testosterone Levels Declined in Last 20 Years," Reuters, January 19, 2007, https://www.reuters.com/article/health-testosterone-levels-dc/mens-testosterone-levels-declined-in-last-20-years-idUKKIM16976320061031.

159   Hadley, *Endocrinology*, 146.

160   M. S. Carmichael et al., "Plasma Oxytocin Increases in the Human Sexual Response," *The Journal of Clinical Endocrinology and Metabolism* 64, no. 1 (1987): 27–31, doi:10.1210/jcem-64-1-27.

161   Hadley, *Endocrinology*, 104.

162   Magon and Kalra, "The Orgasmic History of Oxytocin."

163   Robinson, *Cupid's Poisoned Arrow*, 109.

164   John J. Bromfield, "Seminal Fluid and Reproduction: Much More Than Previously Thought," *Journal of Assisted Reproduction and Genetics* 31, no. 6 (2014): 627–636, doi:10.1007/s10815-014-0243-y.

165   Ibid.

166   Ivan Roitt et al., *Immunology*, 3rd ed. (London: Mosby, 1993), 10.

167   D. H. Owen and D. F. Katz, "A Review of the Physical and Chemical Properties of Human Semen and the Formulation of a Semen Simulant," *Journal of Andrology* 26 (2005): 459–469, https://doi.org/10.2164/jandrol.04104.

168   Napoleon Hill, *Think and Grow Rich* (Lexington, KY: Fortune Publishing Group, 2013), 133.

169   Ashida Kim, *Ninja Book of Enlightenment*. (Lake Alfred, FL: Dojo Press, 2000), 56–57.

170 Śivānanda Swami, *Practice of Brahmacharya*, 13th ed. (Uttar Pradesh, India: Divine Life Society, 2012), 72.

171 Weor, *The Perfect Matrimony*, 42–55.

172 Editors of *Encyclopaedia Britannica*, "Samadhi," *Encyclopaedia Britannica*, February 17 2021, https://www.britannica.com/topic/samadhi-Indian-philosophy.

173 Owen and Katz, "A Review of the Physical and Chemical Properties."

174 Arpád Dobolyi et al., "The Neuroprotective Functions of Transforming Growth Factor Beta Proteins," *International Journal of Molecular Sciences* 13, no. 7 (2012): 8219–8258, doi:10.3390/ijms13078219.

175 Sung-Min Ahn et al., "Human Microglial Cells Synthesize Albumin in Brain," *PloS One* 3, no. 7 (July 30, 2008): e2829, doi:10.1371/journal.pone.0002829; Kanaiyalal D. Prajapati et al., "Current Perspectives on Potential Role of Albumin in Neuroprotection," *Reviews in the Neurosciences* 22, no. 3 (2011): 355–363, doi:10.1515/RNS.2011.028; Ludmila Belayev et al., "Albumin Treatment Reduces Neurological Deficit and Protects Blood-Brain Barrier Integrity after Acute Intracortical Hematoma in the Rat," *Stroke* 36, no. 2 (2005): 326–331, doi:10.1161/01.STR.0000152949.31366.3d.

176 Kathryn M. Lenz and Lars H. Nelson, "Microglia and Beyond: Innate Immune Cells as Regulators of Brain Development and Behavioral Function," *Frontiers in Immunology* 9 (April 2018): 698, doi:10.3389/fimmu.2018.00698; Shannon L. Dean et al., "Prostaglandin E2 Is an Endogenous Modulator of Cerebellar Development and Complex Behavior during a Sensitive Postnatal Period," *The European Journal of Neuroscience* 35, no. 8 (2012): 1218–1229, doi:10.1111/j.1460-9568.2012.08032.x.

177 Snow et al., "Chronic Dietary Creatine"; Hamilton Roschel et al., "Creatine Supplementation and Brain Health," *Nutrients* 13, no. 2 (February 2021): 586, doi:10.3390/nu13020586.

178 Emma Derbyshire and Rima Obeid, "Choline, Neurological Development and Brain Function: A Systematic Review Focusing on the First 1000 Days," *Nutrients* 12, no. 6 (June 2020): 1731, doi:10.3390/nu12061731; S. Y. Chung et al., "Administration of Phosphatidylcholine Increases Brain Acetylcholine Concentration and Improves Memory in Mice with Dementia," *The Journal of Nutrition* 125, no. 6 (1995): 1484–1489, doi:10.1093/jn/125.6.1484.

179 Bing Wang, "Sialic Acid Is an Essential Nutrient for Brain Development and Cognition," *Annual Review of Nutrition* 29 (2009): 177–222, doi:10.1146/annurev.nutr.28.061807.155515.

180   Keisuke Ikegami et al., "Interconnection between Circadian Clocks and Thyroid Function," *Nature Reviews: Endocrinology* 15, no. 10 (2019): 590–600, doi:10.1038/s41574-019-0237-z.

181   Gary Wittert, "The Relationship between Sleep Disorders and Testosterone in Men," *Asian Journal of Andrology* 16, no. 2 (2014): 262–265, doi:10.4103/1008-682X.122586.

182   Tennant, *Healing Is Voltage*, 89–92.

183   Yogi Bhajan, *Foods for Health and Healing: Remedies and Recipes*, ed. Gurubanda Singh Khalsa and Parmatma Singh Khalsa (Santa Cruz, NM: Kundalini Research Institute, 1983), 49.

184   "Masturbation (n.)," Etymology, https://www.etymonline.com/word/masturbation.

185   Ashraf Tashakori et al., "Lessons Learned from the Study of Masturbation and Its Comorbity with Psychiatric Disorders in Children: The First Analytic Study," *Electronic Physician* 9, no. 4 (April 2017): 4096–4100, doi:10.19082/4096.

186   Heitham K. Ajlouni et al., "Infantile and Early Childhood Masturbation: Sex Hormones and Clinical Profile," *Annals of Saudi Medicine* 30, no. 6 (2010): 471–474, doi:10.4103/0256-4947.72271.

187   Margaret M. McCarthy, "Estradiol and the Developing Brain," *Physiological Reviews* 88, no. 1 (2008): 91–124, doi:10.1152/physrev.00010.2007.

188   G. M. McCray, "Excessive Masturbation of Childhood: A Symptom of Tactile Deprivation?," *Pediatrics* 62, no. 3 (1978): 277–279.

189   Andree Brooks, "Divorced Parents and the Neglected Child," *New York Times*, July 28, 1986, https://www.nytimes.com/1986/07/28/style/divorced-parents-and-the-neglected-child.html.

190   Anna-Karin Lennartsson and Ingibjörg H. Jonsdottir, "Prolactin in Response to Acute Psychosocial Stress in Healthy Men and Women," *Psychoneuroendocrinology* 36, no. 10 (2011): 1530–1539, doi:10.1016/j.psyneuen.2011.04.007.

191   Voet and Voet, *Biochemistry*, 511.

192   Hadley, *Endocrinology*, 427.

193   Todd Love et al., "Neuroscience of Internet Pornography Addiction: A Review and Update," *Behavioral Sciences* 5, no, 3 (September 2015): 388–433, doi:10.3390/bs5030388.

194   Zawn Villines, "Porn Addiction: Signs, Causes, and Treatment," *Medical News Today*, February 26, 2021, https://www.medicalnewstoday.com/articles/porn-addiction.

195   Jeffrey Hays, "Taoism and Sex," Facts and Details, September 2021, https://factsanddetails.com/china/cat3/sub10/entry-7540.html.

196   Ibid.

197   Ankita Prasad et al., "Sexual Activity, Endogenous Reproductive Hormones and Ovulation in Premenopausal Women," *Hormones and Behavior* 66, no. 2 (2014): 330–338, doi:10.1016/j.yhbeh.2014.06.012.

198   Adrian V. Jaeggi et al., "Salivary Oxytocin Increases Concurrently with Testosterone and Time Away from Home among Returning Tsimane' Hunters," *Biology Letters* 11, no. 3 (2015): 20150058, doi:10.1098/rsbl.2015.0058.

199   Weor, *The Perfect Matrimony*, 54.

200   M. Petersson et al., "Oxytocin Causes a Sustained Decrease in Plasma Levels of Corticosterone in Rats," *Neuroscience Letters* 264, no. 1–3 (1999): 41–44, doi:10.1016/s0304-3940(99)00159-7.

201   Yael Apter-Levy et al., "Impact of Maternal Depression across the First 6 Years of Life on the Child's Mental Health, Social Engagement, and Empathy: The Moderating Role of Oxytocin," *The American Journal of Psychiatry* 170, no. 10 (2013): 1161–1168, doi:10.1176/appi.ajp.2013.12121597.

202   A. Booth, D. R. Johnson, and D. A. Granger, "Testosterone, Marital Quality, and Role Overload," *Journal of Marriage and Family* 67 (2005): 483–498, https://doi.org/10.1111/j.0022-2445.2005.00130.

203   Alan Booth et al., "Testosterone and Child and Adolescent Adjustment: The Moderating Role of Parent-Child Relationships," *Developmental Psychology* 39, no. 1 (2003): 85–98, doi:10.1037//0012-1649.39.1.85.

204   Jamie L. Hanson et al., "Family Poverty Affects the Rate of Human Infant Brain Growth," *PloS One* 8, no. 12 (December 2013): e80954, doi:10.1371/journal.pone.0080954.

205   Hanson et al., 2013.

206   Hanson et al., 2013.

207   Nicholas Wade, "Your Body Is Younger Than You Think," *New York Times*, August 2, 2005, https://www.nytimes.com/2005/08/02/science/your-body-is-younger-than-you-think.html.

208   William S. Klug et al., *Concepts of Genetics*, 8th ed. (Englewood Cliffs, NJ: Prentice Hall, 2006), 296–301.

209   Walsh, *Nutrient Power*, 37–43.

210   Wade, "Your Body Is Younger Than You Think."

211   Michael Simmons, "Necrosis (Causes of), Inflammation & Apoptosis," YouTube, May 27, 2020, https://www.youtube.com/watch?v=B-Kc6iSS8kM&t=22s].

212   Joseph Murphy, *The Power of Your Subconscious Mind: Unlock Your Master Key to Success* (Radford, VA: Wilder Publications, 2007), 72.

213   Jacob A. Riis, *How the Other Half Lives: Studies among the Tenements of New York* (Mineola, NY: Dover Publications, 1971), 214.

214   "Stock Market 101," TD Bank, https://www.td.com/ca/en/investing/direct-investing/articles/what-is-stock-market.

215   Dayana Yochim and Andrea Coombes, "Roth vs. Traditional IRA: Which Is Right for You?," NerdWallet, January 4, 2023, https://www.nerdwallet.com/article/investing/roth-or-traditional-ira-account.

216   Kevin Voigt and Sabrina Parys, "11 Best Online Stock Brokers for Beginners of February 2023," NerdWallet, November 1, 2022, https://www.nerdwallet.com/best/investing/online-brokers-for-beginners.

217   John C. Bogle, *The Little Book of Common Sense Investing: The Only Way to Guarantee Your Fair Share of Stock Market Returns* (Hoboken, NJ: John Wiley and Sons, 2007), 24.

218   Ibid., 27.

219   Ibid., 34.

220   Ibid., 30.

221   Bogle, *Little Book of Common Sense Investing*, 37; Benjamin Graham, *The Intelligent Investor* (New York: Harper, 2006), 218, 243, 245–246.

222   Graham, *The Intelligent Investor*, 249.

223   Ibid., 29.

224   Ibid., *The Intelligent Investor*, 221.

225   Nicole M. Avena et al., "Evidence for Sugar Addiction: Behavioral and Neurochemical Effects of Intermittent, Excessive Sugar Intake," *Neuroscience and Biobehavioral Reviews* 32, no. 1: 20–39, https://www.ncbi.nlm.nih.gov/pmc/articles/PMC2235907/.

226   Joseph Nguyen, "What Is the Difference between Investing and Speculating?," Investopedia, July 13, 2022, https://www.investopedia.

227   com/ask/answers/09/difference-between-investing-speculating.asp#:~:text=Day%20trading%20is%20a%20form,the%20trading%20session%20is%20complete.

227   Graham, *The Intelligent Investor*, 348, 364–365.

228   Investopedia, https://www.investopedia.com/.

229   Eric Reed, "Shares Outstanding vs. Float: Key Differences," Smartasset, December 9, 2021, https://smartasset.com/investing/shares-outstanding-vs-float.

230   Will Kenton, "Zombies," ed. Amy Drury, Investopedia, August 31, 2021, https://www.investopedia.com/terms/z/zombies.asp.

231   Bogle, *The Little Book of Common Sense Investing*, 17.

232   Graham, *The Intelligent Investor*, 490.

233   Bogle, *The Little Book of Common Sense Investing*, 10.

www.ingramcontent.com/pod-product-compliance
Lightning Source LLC
LaVergne TN
LVHW010200070526
838199LV00062B/4434